D1447099

INTELLECTUAL FREEDOM
FOR TEENS

ALA Editions purchases fund advocacy, awareness, and accreditation programs for library professionals worldwide.

INTELLECTUAL FREEDOM

FOR TEENS

A Practical Guide for Young Adult and School Librarians

EDITED BY

Kristin Fletcher-Spear
and Kelly Tyler

A YALSA Publication

ala
editions

AN IMPRINT OF THE AMERICAN LIBRARY ASSOCIATION
CHICAGO | 2014

Kristin Fletcher-Spear is the administrative librarian at the Foothills Branch Library in Glendale, Arizona. She is coauthor of *Library Collections for Teens: Manga and Graphic Novels* and has written for YALSA, VOYA, and Library Media Connection. She earned her master's degree in library science at Indiana University.

Kelly Tyler is the branch manager for the Van Nuys Branch at the Los Angeles Public Library. Prior to becoming a supervisor, she worked as a youth services librarian and was a mentor and trainer for new teen librarians. This is her first book.

© 2014 by the American Library Association

Printed in the United States of America

18 17 16 15 14   5 4 3 2 1

Extensive effort has gone into ensuring the reliability of the information in this book; however, the publisher makes no warranty, express or implied, with respect to the material contained herein.

ISBNs
978-0-8389-1200-3 (paper)
978-0-8389-1252-2 (PDF)
978-0-8389-1253-9 (ePub)
978-0-8389-1254-6 (Kindle)

Library of Congress Cataloging-in-Publication Data
Intellectual freedom for teens : a practical guide for young adult and school librarians / edited by
    Kristin Fletcher-Spear and Kelly Tyler.
        pages   cm
        "A YALSA publication."
        Includes bibliographical references and index.
        ISBN 978-0-8389-1200-3 (alk. paper)
        1. Young adults libraries—Censorship—United States. 2. School libraries—Censorship—
United States. 3. Intellectual freedom—United States. 4. Prohibited books—United States. I.
Fletcher-Spear, Kristin, editor of compilation. II. Tyler, Kelly, editor of compilation.
    Z718.5.I58 2014
    027.62'6—dc23   2013051234

Cover design by Kimberly Thornton. Images © Shutterstock, Inc. Text design by Pauline Neuwirth, Neuwirth & Associates, Inc. in the ITC New Baskerville Std and Helvetica Neu LT std typefaces.

♾ This paper meets the requirements of ANSI/NISO Z39.48–1992 (Permanence of Paper).

DEFIANCE PUBLIC LIBRARY

JUN 2 9 2016

CONTENTS

DEFIANCE PUBLIC LIBRARY

ACKNOWLEDGMENTS

I DEDICATE THIS TO my mom, Kay Fletcher, who gave me the foundation that fostered my passion of intellectual freedom. I thank Howard Rosenbaum at Indiana University. Without his intellectual freedom course at Indiana University, I would have floundered in the IF issues I've had in my career. Jason, thank you for all the love and support. You and our kids are my life. *—Kristin*

Ken, you are my partner in life and work. Thank you for giving me time, your keen librarian's eye for detail, and boundless moral support while I was working on this book and my many other projects that don't offer an opportunity for me to show you public gratitude. Without you and Julian, life would be dull indeed. *—Kelly*

We also thank the authors who contributed chapters to this guide. Their expertise in their areas are what made them perfect candidates for their chapters: Stevie, Linda, and Karen, thank you for your dedication to this title and to teen library services.

—Kristin and Kelly

INTRODUCTION

Mary K. Chelton

I AM PLEASED TO see not only a new, updated edition of what should probably be considered a YA-professional classic, but also that the authors have taken an issue-oriented, contextual approach, recognizing both the similarities and differences between school and public libraries. It could have been easy to list all the titles of interest to young adults that have been challenged over the years, along with their reviews. This would have only perpetuated the myth that reviews can somehow "save" librarians under challenge or attack by censors. Often the title being challenged has never been reviewed with the YA audience in mind, or the age ranges for the title suggested by the reviewer do not support the age of the user on whose behalf the challenge is being made. In fact, the variation and possible inaccuracy in suggested age ranges across library review media could almost be viewed as an indirect contributor to challenges. Reviews may support the fact that the decision to purchase something for the collection that upsets the challenger was not arbitrary, but they are good for little else.

Chapter 2 looks particularly valuable, not only because it covers the open "dirty little secret" of self-censorship—that is, not buying something you know the young adults would love because you do not want to get yourself in trouble. One can always sense an urge to self-censor when YA librarians start talking about appropriateness for the YA collection. This happens frequently with graphic novels, for example. Separate YA collections attract attention, which is what they are supposed to do for YAs, but disapproving adults and colleagues also notice what is in them; hence the concern over "appropriateness," or in the school context, "age-appropriateness." These discussions frequently attempt to sound like literary criticism, when they are really about political fear. I ran into this once with a seventh grade teacher who participated in a discussion of *Sold* by Patricia McCormick that I was leading for a local library system. Everyone in the group, including the squirming teacher (the only nonlibrarian in the group) who kept bringing up appropriateness, agreed that the book had an important theme (sexual trafficking), that kids would be interested in and like it, and that kids could read it, so I pointed out that this was a political problem, not an appropriateness problem. The urge to self-censor is probably as strong as the urge to run for the hills when challenged, but because it is often hard to predict what item, specifically, will set someone off, doing it for one title may just be self-defeating in some other way and may inevitably lead to a delusional complacency over challenges.

The necessity of having a materials selection policy should go without saying, but there are still librarians who feel that, if they do not let anyone know what they are doing, they can get away with it in perpetuity. Hammering out a policy that should include, among other provisions, how one purchases possibly controversial material for teens, and how the community can challenge items in the collection, is a clarifying professional exercise and usually quite helpful in explaining librarian decision making to the public (if it is not filed in a drawer immediately upon completion, which is often the case, or lost in a huge procedural manual). A selection policy should be immediately handy and available when staff members need to refer to it or use it in discussions with users.

Another use for the policy is in staff training, which the authors discuss in a section called "Preparing Staff for Questions and Potential Challenges." If a library's commitment to intellectual freedom is to succeed, the entire staff needs to be on board, from the janitor to the library/school board chair. It can be scary to be on the receiving end of an angry or upset challenger, especially if the staff member agrees with the objections presented, so there has to be lots of behind-the-scenes discussion and practice for responding interpersonally, as well as understanding when to refer a challenger to a higher level staff member, when to use a request for reconsideration form, or how to get the right tone into a written response. Intellectual freedom needs to be managed in such a way that it is part of the fabric of everyday library practice, not an occasional exercise in crisis management.

I have often said that, if it means the difference between having something available and being forced to censor it because of objections to the cover, take the cover off and keep the book. While I consider myself to be an intellectual freedom purist, meaning that people, regardless of age, should be able to pursue their interests in libraries without interference, the real world often does not allow it. One looks for the best pragmatic compromises, so I look forward to the potential solutions section in chapter 3 which will, no doubt, cover the "tap on the shoulder" of users viewing graphic sex on unfiltered computers, the ethics of temporary reserve shelves and parenting collections, and the joys of managing DVD collections for young adults rated by the Motion Picture Association of America. The American Library Association (ALA) Office for Intellectual Freedom (OIF) has vast information available on promulgating intellectual freedom in libraries as well as on what to do when something happens in the trenches of real life. OIF is prominent in the list of important resources provided in this book.

It does no good to resist challenges if nobody knows either that something has been challenged or that you have resisted it, so I am glad to see that marketing and programming are included in chapter 4. Because intellectual freedom seems an abstraction until censorship happens to you personally, many teens who have never experienced it this way need practice thinking about it as new abstract thinking abilities develop. One of the most famous of these YA think-about-it programs was the human chain symbolizing chained books that Cathie Dunn Macrae's (former editor of *Voice of Youth Advocates*) Young Adult Advisory Committee did at the Boulder (Colorado) Public Library some years back. They also went to the trouble of writing a play about censorship, only to be banned from performing it after being booked in several local schools. I suspect few of them consider intellectual freedom to be an abstraction anymore.

Because the Internet and cell phones are ubiquitous in YA life now, I am glad to see that social networking success stories are included, especially since Facebook has become so contentious in terms of privacy issues, both among teens themselves and between teens and adults. Intellectual freedom now covers much more than just challenges to collection items.

If the existence of this book does nothing more than help YA librarians think better about troubling intellectual freedom issues with more clarity buoyed by increased intestinal fortitude, it will have done its job. I do think, however, that it should also stand as a reminder that *the* most important issue in YA services is still remembering *who* the primary client is, namely, the young adult. To serve young adults well, YA librarians need to be street smart and politically savvy about intellectual freedom issues. This book goes a long way in helping them do that. Otherwise, they stand the risk of being paralyzed because they are looking over their shoulders constantly for real and imaginary censors.

INTELLECTUAL FREEDOM AND YOUNG ADULT LIBRARIANSHIP
An Overview

N 1999 TOM REYNOLDS asked readers of *Alki*, the Washington Library Association's journal, to consider what age group is most affected by intellectual freedom issues:

> The answer . . . is teenagers. Take a look at ALA's list of the most frequently challenged or banned books . . . . What do these eighty titles have in common? Most are either written for or are popular with teen readers, or are of such literary value that they regularly appear on high school reading lists.[1]

He also questions the wisdom of withholding digital content from minors, explaining that libraries have a responsibility to teach young adults how to use the Internet rather than blocking material that may be questionable.

Reynolds's article, with updates to some of the names and dates, could have been written now, more than a decade later. In 2011 seven of the top ten most challenged books, based on instances reported to the ALA's OIF, were written for teens (and strong argument could be made to consider an eighth, *To Kill a Mockingbird*, in that category).[2] The Children's Internet Protection Act (CIPA): passed in 2001, "imposes certain types of requirements on any school or library that receives funding for Internet access or internal connections from the E-rate program."[3] Those requirements often mean filtering, but also mandate that schools create Internet safety policies and educate students on how to safely and smartly navigate content online. Privacy, whether learning how to maintain it on social networking sites or ensuring that a teen's borrowing history remains known to that teen only, is another aspect of intellectual freedom for YA library staff to consider.

"Society and libraries vacillate between allowing YAs to behave responsibly while at the same time wanting to protect them," Patrick Jones, Michele Gorman, and Tricia Suellentrop noted in 2004, hitting at the very heart of what makes defining intellectual freedom for young adults so tricky for parents and educators as well as library staff.[4] In the Library Bill of Rights, ALA argues that libraries should offer materials on all viewpoints, challenge censorship, and ensure that each person's right to accessing all library materials is open and not prevented by race, religion, or age, among other factors. But the profession's ideals do not always match up with those espoused by governments and school boards, political groups, or individuals. This is where a school librarian, YA librarian, or library worker's expertise in protecting teens' freedom to read and ability to access material online is most important.

DEFINING INTELLECTUAL FREEDOM

Intellectual freedom, broadly speaking, is an individual's right to seek out information of any kind and enjoy the free expression of ideas and information. It is the foundation of democracy and a cornerstone of librarianship.

In the context of librarianship, intellectual freedom is sometimes seen simply as fighting against banning books or challenging libraries' ability to keep certain items in their collections. While challenges and book bans are the more highly charged or visible aspects of intellectual freedom, to limit the definition to challenges and book banning is highly reductive.

Carrying controversial materials and defending a young adult's right to access them do likely rank highly in a teen librarian's intellectual freedom priorities. But library staff who work with teens may find themselves defending the rights of their patrons beyond materials: they may need to argue in favor of teens' ability to hang out in the library's public computer lab after school or the right to privacy, explaining to parents that they cannot see a list of materials recently borrowed by their children; school librarians may need to explain to administrators why the school should consider unblocking You-Tube for educational use during the Young Adult Library Services Association (YALSA) Teen Tech Week. Intellectual freedom within libraries has grown to include the rights of library patrons to access digital content on library computers, to have their checkout records maintained privately, to enjoy the same access to public spaces within a library, all no matter a patron's age, personal political view-points, race, or religion, among other factors. It can also mean examining whether a library self-censors by deciding not to collect materials that could engender controversy or undue attention. This book intends to offer guidance and consideration to the ever-expanding universe of intellectual freedom for teen library staff and school librarians.

ALA AND INTELLECTUAL FREEDOM

The Library Bill of Rights was first published by ALA in 1939 and has been amended six times. ALA's commitment to intellectual freedom issues is stated clearly and plainly within:

The American Library Association affirms that all libraries are forums for information and ideas, and that the following basic policies should guide their services.

Books and other library resources should be provided for the interest, information, and enlightenment of all people of the community the library serves. Materials should not be excluded because of the origin, background, or views of those contributing to their creation.

Libraries should provide materials and information presenting all points of view on current and historical issues. Materials should not be proscribed or removed because of partisan or doctrinal disapproval.

Libraries should challenge censorship in the fulfillment of their responsibility to provide information and enlightenment.

Libraries should cooperate with all persons and groups concerned with resisting abridgment of free expression and free access to ideas.

A person's right to use a library should not be denied or abridged because of origin, age, background, or views.

Libraries that make exhibit spaces and meeting rooms available to the public they serve should make such facilities available on an equitable basis, regardless of the beliefs or affiliations of individuals or groups requesting their use.

Adopted June 19, 1939, by the ALA Council; amended October 14, 1944; June 18, 1948; February 2, 1961; June 27, 1967; January 23, 1980; inclusion of "age" reaffirmed January 23, 1996.[5]

Given the profession's commitment to supporting intellectual freedom, ALA created OIF in 1967, charging it with "implementing ALA policies concerning the concept of intellectual freedom as embodied in the Library Bill of Rights, the Association's basic policy on free access to libraries and library materials."[6] OIF's mission remains educating libraries and the general public about intellectual freedom and the important role that it plays in libraries. Led by Judith Krug until her death in 2009 and currently led by Barbara Jones, OIF collects statistics about intellectual freedom, particularly challenges, and offers support and resources for library staff handling intellectual freedom issues. In addition, OIF publishes *The Intellectual Freedom Manual,* soon to be in its ninth edition; creates toolkits to aid library staff in understanding intellectual freedom issues; and sponsors Banned Books Week, a celebration founded in 1982 by Krug to honor authors and books that faced censorship and to draw attention to the First Amendment.

In 1969 ALA established the Freedom to Read Foundation (FTRF) as a First Amendment legal defense fund, although the foundation does more than support librarians and libraries embroiled in free speech–related litigation. FTRF is directly involved in legal cases, both as plaintiff and amicus, and defends library customers by arguing against access to confidential records at the library. In addition, FTRF offers legal and financial help, including grants, to libraries, librarians, and other literary professionals (including publishers, authors, booksellers, journalists, and others) facing attempts to restrict materials and services. FTRF is an affiliate of ALA but works closely with the organization.

INTELLECTUAL FREEDOM FOR YOUNG ADULTS

In the same year that ALA founded OIF, its members debated whether intellectual freedom applied to children and teen library users during a preconference event in San Francisco. More than 400 librarians attended the session, "Intellectual Freedom and the Teenager." Panelist Edgar Z. Friedenberg was emphatic that those under 18 deserved the same rights as any other library visitor: "The library is just one more place where kids are taught they are second-class citizens. They learn this . . . from the very atmosphere of the place."[7] Preconference attendees agreed strongly with Friedenberg, enough that age was added as an area of concern to the next revision of the Library Bill of Rights. American courts have also found that minors should be allowed First Amendment protections, although not quite as many as those over the age of 18. The U.S. Supreme Court has argued over the years that minors must have access to "a broad range of information for intellectual growth," arguing that "students 'do not shed their constitutional rights . . . at the schoolhouse gate'" and "'[p]eople are unlikely to become well-functioning, independent-minded adults and responsible citizens if they are raised in an intellectual bubble.'"[8]

Even with these legal protections and the generally supportive view of library staff, minors still face roadblocks to content at the library, school or public, including the removal or restriction of print materials and the filtering of online content.

CHALLENGES AND THE YA LIBRARIAN

Intellectual freedom plays an important role in the professional lives of YA librarians and school librarians because the vast majority of challenges to materials and access is aimed at those under 18. OIF maintains a database of challenges, tracking the number of challenges per year, the reasons for challenges, the initiators of challenges, and the types of institutions in which a challenge takes place. Since 1990 OIF has logged nearly 11,000 challenges; more than 60 percent of them were originated by a parent, with more than two-thirds of challenges taking place in schools or school libraries.[9]

A book challenge is a form of censorship and can lead to a ban, but it is important not to use these terms interchangeably. Challenges and book banning are facets of censorship, which cuts a far broader swath against intellectual freedom than the facets alone. Censorship is a systematic approach to preventing speech that may be considered objectionable. A challenge is a "formal, written complaint, filed with a library or school requesting that materials be removed because of content or appropriateness," and OIF only tracks those challenges that are reported to them or seen in the news; they assume that as many as four or five incidents occur for every one that is reported or covered by media.[10] For a book to be considered banned, it must be removed from a library. Each year, OIF compiles a list of the most frequently challenged books, drawn from challenges reported to them. Approximately 300 to 500 challenges are reported to OIF each year, and it is fair to assume that many of them begin in either the children's or teens' department.

Challenges are launched for a variety of reasons and are not limited to any side of the political spectrum. *Huckleberry Finn* and *To Kill a Mockingbird* have been challenged for offensive language by left-leaning individuals and organizations over their use of the word *nigger*; the picture book *And Tango Makes Three* is one of the most challenged books in the United States over its depiction of two penguins as being gay, even though it contains no sexually suggestive or explicit content. Challenges are aimed at books that are currently breathtakingly popular (The Hunger Games and Harry Potter series) or are older or more obscure (*The Summer of My German Soldier*, originally published in 1973, appeared on the 2001 most-challenged list).[11] The most oft-cited reason for challenging materials is sexually explicit content, followed by offensive language, and "unsuited to age group," according to OIF. It is worth noting, however, that the fourth most popular reason for challenging materials is "other."

Challenges take place in all kinds of libraries and come from a variety of sources. The stereotypical challenge begins with an agitated, organized group or an irate parent, but it can originate from any source. YA specialists can talk about books that individual patrons have suggested be added to a restricted area rather than the YA section, or when a colleague from another department expressed shock that the YA section offered a display of books about extreme sports, as they suggested risky behavior to teen patrons. Ask any school librarian. and she is sure to discuss the limitations that her principal or a colleague has tried to place on materials in her library. In fact, schools often face challenges that go beyond something a parent, student, administrator, or staff member does not want to see on the library shelves. Many classes have required reading lists, and secondary schools often send students home for the summer accompanied by a reading list. Objections are often made against titles on those reading lists, be they classics or more modern releases.

Challenges cannot be avoided. No matter how careful a library believes it can be, someone somewhere is going to take offense to the materials that a library collects (or chooses not to collect). Even librarians who engage in self-censorship—an ongoing, little-discussed approach in which libraries, particularly those that serve large young adult populations, opt not to collect materials of great popularity or literary merit that are likely to garner complaints—cannot ward off potential challenges. A 2009 *School Library Journal* study found that as many as 70 percent of the school librarians they surveyed engaged in self-censorship because of concerns that parents may object, yet nearly half (49 percent) admitted to facing a challenge situation in the library.[12]

How is a librarian to cope with these odds? Well, as the old saying goes, the best offense is a good defense, and librarians will find many stellar defenses in chapter 2, which details how a library and its staff can prepare themselves by creating a materials selection policy and delineating a formal policy for addressing library patron complaints and challenges. And chapter 3 provides guidance for handling a challenge from both internal and external audiences and defending the library publicly.

OTHER INTELLECTUAL FREEDOM ISSUES FOR TEEN LIBRARY PATRONS

Challenges and removals of physical materials are the most visible threat to intellectual freedom for teens, but content filtering and ignoring minors' right to privacy are significant issues for teen librarians to consider as well. CIPA requires libraries to implement an Internet safety policy. Those libraries who receive E-rate discounts, Library Services and Technology Act grant funds, or funding under title III of the Elementary and Secondary Education Act must filter or block "illegal visual depictions accessible on the Internet."[13] Although CIPA ostensibly applies only to obscene content, pornography, and speech that is not protected constitutionally, many filters block content so broadly that they restrict minors' ability to access constitutionally protected speech online. In addition, many libraries and school districts use CIPA as a reason to block social networking and gaming sites, despite the law not requiring them to do so and research that shows that youth benefit from exposure and instruction in using these sites responsibly.[14]

Librarians need to be advocates for teens when it comes to the Internet, championing the positive outcomes of social networking and gaming and offering instruction on how to be smart, ethical users of technology. As social networking has grown in the past few years, library privacy concerns have grown to include teaching teens about what content is appropriate to share online and what should be kept private. And, in the age of torrenting and remixing content online, teens need to learn the importance of properly using—or not using—others' copyrighted materials. How can society expect teens to learn that downloading music without paying for it is often illegal, if they are not given the opportunity to do so?

One important tool working in libraries' favor is the U.S. Broadband Data Improvement Act of 2008. As part of that legislation, schools and libraries that receive E-rate funding are required to teach students how to behave online, including how to safely use social networking sites and chat rooms, as well as how to be aware of and handle cyberbullying. In addition, libraries can take advantage of events like YALSA's Teen Tech Week, an annual celebration of technology and teens at the library, which offers an excellent opportunity for schools and libraries to safely explore the importance of open access to teens with parents, guardians, educators, and administrators. Chapter 5 further explores intellectual freedom online and how librarians and educators can further stand up for teens' rights online.

Privacy and ethical use of online information is a major intellectual freedom issue for library patrons, and teens are no exception. Privacy at the library includes a teen's right to check out materials that he wants to, with input from a parent or guardian; it also includes a teen's right to have her library records kept confidential. A parent who needs to pay late fees may innocently ask to see a teen's checkout history to make sure the charges are correct. While this is often done benevolently, there may be materials that a teen has checked out that she does not want a parent to see and, in some cases, it may be important that a parent not know about, such as in suspicion of abuse. This is an ethical issue that comes up repeatedly, and likely will, as long as teens see the library as a place where they can find answers to sometimes difficult questions. Librarians need to be prepared to deal with difficult conversations, and it helps to integrate a privacy policy into a library's guiding documents.

CONCLUSION

There is a fine line between teaching responsibility and protecting youths from those materials that may not be appropriate for them. That line, many librarians believe, should be set by the young adult, with input from the young person's family, not a government entity or a concerned citizen. Unfortunately, many government entities and concerned citizens feel otherwise, and those efforts are often focused on teens.

As librarians, it is important to remember that our responsibility is ultimately to teen patrons, to ensure that the library remains a safe space for them to meet their informational needs, whether it is finding statistics online to support a high school research paper, a magazine to entertain them, or the answers to difficult questions about the turbulent world in which they live. By ensuring that they can trust the library to help them find whatever they need, in whatever materials are appropriate, without judgment, we can ensure that they continue to find the library a necessary resource.

NOTES

1. Tom Reynolds. "A Place to Explore, Think, and Grow: Will Libraries Meet the Intellectual Freedom Needs of Students in the 21st Century?" *Alki: The Journal* of *the Washington Library Association* 15, no. 3 (1999): 25.

2. "Frequently Challenged Books of the 21st Century: 2011," American Library Association, accessed June 22, 2012, www.ala.org/advocacy/banned/frequentlychallenged/21stcenturychallenged.

3. "Children's Internet Protection Act," Federal Communications Commission, accessed June 22, 2012, www.fcc.gov/guides/childrens-internet-protection-act.

4. Patrick Jones, Michele Gorman, and Tricia Suellentrop, *Connecting Young Adults and Libraries: A How to Do It Manual*, 3rd ed. (New York: Neal-Schuman, 2004): 335.

5. "Library Bill of Rights," American Library Association, accessed June 22, 2012, www.ala.org/advocacy/intfreedom/librarybill.

6. "Mission," American Library Association Office for Intellectual Freedom, accessed July 20, 2012, www.ala.org/offices/oif.

7. "Number of Challenges by Year, Reason, Initiator, and Institution, 1990–2010," American Library Association Office for Intellectual Freedom, accessed June 22, 2012, www.ala.org/advocacy/banned/frequentlychallenged/stats.

8. *Tinker v. Des Moines Independent Community School District*, 393 U.S. 503, 506, 511 (1969); *AAMA v. Kendrick*, 244 F.3d 572, 577 (7th Cir. 2001).

9. American Library Association Office for Intellectual Freedom, *Intellectual Freedom Manual*, 8th ed. (Chicago: ALA, 2010): 351.

10. "About Banned & Challenged Books," American Library Association Office for Intellectual Freedom, accessed June 22, 2012, www.ala.org/advocacy/banned/aboutbannedbooks.

11. "Frequently Challenged Books of the 21st Century," American Library Association Office for Intellectual Freedom, accessed June 22, 2012, www.ala.org/advocacy/banned/frequentlychallenged/21stcenturychallenged.

12. Debra Lau Whelan, "A Dirty Little Secret: Self-Censorship," *School Library Journal* (February 1, 2009), www.schoollibraryjournal.com/article/CA6632974.html.

13. ALA OIF, Intellectual Freedom Manual, 40.

14. Ibid.

BEFORE A CHALLENGE OCCURS
How to Prepare Yourself and Your Staff

Kristin Fletcher-Spear

NOW THAT WE have a firm understanding of intellectual freedom and the importance of digital access, we are going to delve into the practical side of things. Developing formal procedures, training and educating staff and officials such as school and library boards about said procedures and intellectual freedom, and perhaps the part most libraries tend to forget—maintaining a strong presence and support within the community that you serve—are all fundamental to protecting intellectual freedoms in libraries. Even though challenges and complaints will occur in all types of libraries, there are several things we, as teen and school librarians, can do to help prepare our libraries and staff before a challenge ever occurs. In this chapter we are going to cover the following topics:

- ▶ Developing a Materials Selection Policy
- ▶ Creating a Library User Complaint Procedure
- ▶ Preparing Staff for Questions and Potential Challenges
- ▶ Collection Development, Collection Management, and Self-Censorship

DEVELOPING A MATERIALS SELECTION POLICY

Having a strong materials policy in place will not necessarily stop library user complaints, but it will encourage stability and continuity in the library's operations.[1] It also allows users to see that the library has thought out the materials selection for the library and that the library is willing to be accountable to the policy. A materials selection policy is also sometimes called a collection development statement. This policy should be based on your library's mission statement. One example is the library system in Glendale, Arizona. Glendale Public Library's statement begins with a brief description of the city and the library's mission statement: "The Glendale Public Library is a service-oriented organization, whose primary responsibility is to provide free and equal access without prejudice or discrimination to each man, woman, and child in the community."[2]

Your library's mission statement will be the basis of all your policy making, whether it be on materials selection, programming, service goals, or the like. The next step in drafting the materials statement is to describe the goals of the library's collection. For example, a teen department may say in its goal for teen materials that the non-fiction collection is meant to be a recreational reading collection rather than a homework assistance collection. A materials selection statement should describe who is responsible for the collection (i.e., professional staffs, a collection development team or coordinator, etc.). It should expand on the selection process with the general criteria used to determine purchasing. It should also cover deselection briefly and gift donations. Some libraries do not specify types of materials, rather placing the various materials all together. There are positives to this, such as not needing to update your policy every time a new technology or material type emerges. For example, a general policy may cover graphic novels and e-books without calling them by name. It also allows for the argument that all the materials are equal in the eyes of the library staff and one particular type does not need to be called out to protect it better than another type. Other libraries choose to be specific in their policies. This ensures that their policies are updated more frequently, that they are more thorough in the case of a challenge or complaint, and that the material type is better protected. The final section of a materials selection statement should explain the procedure for a challenge or a complaint on materials or access to said materials.

As teen librarians who work in a public library system that already has a materials statement in place, you may be wondering what this entails for you. You need to be familiar with your current policy for several reasons:

- ▶ Knowing your policy enables you to discuss intellectually your collection when a concerned patron approaches.
- ▶ Your policy should direct your library's goals and what materials you select for your teen collection.
- ▶ As a teen librarian, you are the advocacy voice for teens in your community. If the policy does not reflect the teens' needs, then it is up to you to lead the way to change.

When I began overseeing the teen collections development in my library system, I first created a materials selection policy that was specific to just the teen materials. Although this was in no way an official document and if there was a patron complaint I would have used my library's procedure. Having a specific policy for teen items helped me keep a firm grasp of what was collected and how it was collected in the department. This aided other staff members when we started the graphic novel collection. Because there were few professional journals reviewing graphic novels at that time, the teen department materials policy specifically mentioned how we would evaluate the graphic novels that had not received professional reviews. Do not assume that your library system has a materials policy even if it has been established for decades. There are many public libraries that do not have one established and only when a complaint arises do they realize the need for one.

School librarians have a stronger need to be vigilant about ensuring that the policies are written, approved by the school board, and kept current. According to the ALA's OIF, 69 percent of challenges in the past twenty years have occurred in schools and school libraries.[3] When creating a school media center's materials policy, you must investigate what has already been created by your school administration and board of education. The administration may have laid the foundation of the media center's goals in their policies and procedures. The individual media center should reflect these procedures but still lay out the materials policy within terms of intellectual freedom and access to materials. School media policies can work this information in different ways. Plainview School in DeKalb County,

Alabama, refers to the administrative policies in its policy statement.[4] By giving the mission statement of the county's public school system, then the school's mission statement, and finally the Plainview School Library Media Program's mission, the library media center has positioned the hierarchy in clear and understandable terms. Each mission statement complements the others while still being specific to its organization. While Plainview's policy on collections and challenges only states that a committee would be called in the event of a challenge as described in the DeKalb County Schools policies, other schools' policies may go into the process step-by-step. For example, the Adair County R-I School District in Novinger, Missouri, has a comprehensive account in their Library Media Center Handbook laying out the reconsideration process in minute detail that allows for transparency.[5] As a school media specialist, it will be your role to make sure the policies are up to date and champion both the students' needs in curriculum and their intellectual freedom rights in the media center.

CREATING A LIBRARY USER COMPLAINT PROCEDURE

Once the materials selection policy is in place, a library needs to have a procedure set for when a library user has a complaint. While having a materials selection policy does help defuse potential complaints, complaints will still occur. Having a well-written library user complaint procedure, including a patron complaint form, in place *before* a complaint happens has several advantages to it:

▶ It will reduce the confusion about the procedures among staff.[6]
▶ The staff member will have less panic when confronted by a patron.
▶ The form asks the patron for their objections in logical, unemotional terms.
▶ The complaining patron will feel that they are being heard and their objections will be considered seriously.[7]

Handling any library complaint needs to done in a calm and courteous manner. The complainants need to know that their concern is being taken seriously and that the library is interested in hearing from their constituents. Remember that the library user bringing the complaint is practicing their democratic right to be involved in the government.[8]

A procedure for a library complaint should address the different levels of complaints. The first level is an expression of concern, which means that inquiry with judgmental overtones has been made.[9] An example of this may be something like "Is it true you allow children to check out explicit lyric CDs?" The next level is an oral complaint that challenges the presence or appropriateness of the material.[10] This is when a library user says he does not think an item belongs in the library collection. To continue the example, it might sound like "There is no reason to have Eminem CDs where kids could get them." When the user does not receive the response she desires orally, she may choose to put the complaint into writing. This is a formal complaint. Libraries should have a form for concerned users and staff to use. This form most commonly is called a Statement of Concern or a Reconsideration Form.

The Statement of Concern form should have the following components:[11]

- ▶ complainant's contact information
- ▶ who the complainant represents
- ▶ what type of resource and its identifying information
- ▶ how the complainant found out about the resource
- ▶ whether the complainant has read or viewed the resource in its entirety
- ▶ what concerns the complainant has about the resource
- ▶ what other resources the complainant suggests for more information or viewpoints on the topic

Let us look at each component. The *complainant's contact information* is obviously needed so that the staff can respond to them. *Who the complainant represents* is to find out if the complainant is part of an organization or representing himself. A complaint with the power of an organization behind it can have bigger repercussions than one single voice. *What type of resource and its identifying information* is a check sheet of different resources, such as book, magazine, newspaper, CD,

DVD, electronic, website, library program, and other. The resource's information can be as basic as title and author or URL of a website. *How the complainant found out about the resource* will let the staff know if the patron stumbled upon the material at the library or heard about the material elsewhere and decided to act. *Whether the complainant has read or viewed the resource in its entirety* is a standard question because to truly evaluate material one needs to read or view it in its entirety. This lets the library know immediately if the complaint is due to a portion of the resource (e.g., one line or image) versus the material as a whole. Many times libraries will make one of their criteria for dealing with complaints that the complainant must read or view it completely before the library will take the complaint seriously. While that puts the onus on the complainant to do their due diligence and may deter some complaints, it also adds a barrier to having the library user feel heard and taken seriously. *What concerns the complainant has about the resource* is fairly self-explanatory. A library cannot assume what may concern an individual about an item. It is helpful to ask the complainant to comment on the resource as a whole as well as to be specific about the immediate concerns. *What other resources the complainant suggests for more information or viewpoints on the topic* is helpful to have on the statement of concern for controversial nonfiction topics such as evolution and creationism.

PREPARING STAFF FOR QUESTIONS AND POTENTIAL CHALLENGES

The best line of defense is a well-informed staff. For staff members to understand the fundamentals of intellectual freedom and the policies and procedures of the library, staff training will be required. It is important to remember that the majority of library staff members have not studied intellectual freedom and libraries. Without training, the staff will likely end up sending mixed messages to the public. For example, the fairly standard policy of not keeping a record of every title a patron has ever checked out has been explained by untrained staff members as a lack of storage capacity issue rather than the privacy issue it truly is. To begin training, you must first decide what type of training you will want to hold for your library and get the administration's approval and backing. With the support of the library's administration, staff members will likely be more willing to buy into the training than without this support. If you are doing the training, you will have to decide if you are doing training for a single department, like the circulation department, or if you would rather do training for the whole library at one time. Both types of training can be valuable to the attendees. If you target a department, you can deal with specific issues that department may encounter. Training the whole library at once can open the eyes of other departments to issues that may occur in other areas of the library. The decision may lie within your comfort zone as a facilitator or the size of your library.

To begin a training session, one should go over what intellectual freedom is and what the library's role is to protect it. If there is enough time to delve into the history beginning with the First Amendment providing freedom of speech, feel free to do so. Most staff members are not going to want a history lesson to go on too long though, so keep it brief. Here are the historical fundamentals to remember:

▶ The First Amendment protects freedom of speech—this includes the right to freely receive information.
▶ The public library has been legally designated as a limited public forum. This means that it is a "place for access to free and open communication subject to reasonable restrictions as to the time, place, and manner for doing so."[12]
▶ Library users who file a complaint are doing so under their First Amendment rights—the right "to petition the government for a redress of grievances."[13]

Once the history lesson is complete, the next step is going over the policies and procedures of your particular library. You will want to discuss the materials selection policy and the procedure for dealing with complaints, but you may also want to cover your library's mission statement, Internet usage policy, patron confidentiality, and meeting room policies. Each of these policies and procedures covers intellectual freedom within a library. For example, the libraries I have worked at have had very different Internet policies as they pertained to pornography viewing. Understanding the reasoning behind each policy enabled me to best handle situations as they arose. Looking at the policies with the group will bring people's perspectives around the topic. You may find out that a policy is in need of updating.

Most user complaints are ethical dilemmas. Ethical dilemmas are not between right and wrong values, but between two rights. For example, a patron who wishes to restrict access to music with explicit lyrics to only adults may be trying to protect children's innocence and safety. The library that allows open access to the music is protecting freedom of speech for all the community. Having a discussion with staff members about how libraries instill values on both sides of an ethical dilemma may help those staff members who are struggling with library policy issues that they may not personally like.[14]

When a library user issues a complaint, a staff member will most likely have a fight-or-flight response. Professional detachment is key to helping staff handle a library user who may or may not be irate. Maintaining this can be difficult to do under the pressure of the situation, but these handy reminders may help:

1. Step back and breathe deeply.
2. It is not about you.
3. It is not about the person making the challenge.
4. Actively listen.

Each step will help staff keep the challenge neutral, which will help staff respond rationally and effectively.[15] By not making the challenge personal, we refrain from judgment. Reminding ourselves that the user is practicing her democratic rights by complaining to the library may help us to appreciate her viewpoint and concern for the library. Just because we listen to a patron's concerns does not mean we will be bowing to her demands.

Every library user interaction is a customer service opportunity—even when the user is issuing a complaint. Our goal is for the user to leave the library satisfied—even when we cannot do everything for them. For example, when we tell a patron why we cannot label materials for sexual content, we can tell him about resources that will help him determine the content of materials. In *Defending Access with Confidence*, a staff training module, by Catherine Lord lays out a five-point strategy for resolving challenges called LIGHT:

▶ **L**isten and acknowledge the library user's concerns.

▶ **I**nquire if the user would like to discuss it and what they would like done.

▶ **G**ive/Offer explanations, policies, referral to other staff, and "added value" customer service.

▶ **H**elp the user by stating what the library can offer and provide a Statement of Concern form if interested.

▶ **T**hank the patron for caring to express their freedom of speech.[16]

Training staff on these fundamental tools will alleviate much stress when a situation actually occurs. Giving staff the knowledge of the policies and the philosophy behind those policies will give the library staff a stronger sense of intellectual freedom and is well worth the time.

COLLECTION DEVELOPMENT, COLLECTION MANAGEMENT, AND SELF-CENSORSHIP

The last section of this chapter will look at the issue of collection development, the management of said collection, and self-censorship. As stated before, your policies should dictate the appearance and management of your collections. Opponents in challenges have stated that librarians who do collection development censor every time they choose one book over another. That is completely not true and is a misleading conception about collection development. Yes, librarians have to choose between different materials because libraries have finite resources and finite shelf space. Using our collection development policies as the backbone of our collections helps to develop strong, worthwhile collections for our communities. These materials should be well-rounded and have something for every type of reader within our communities. For a teen collection, this means having something for the twelve-year-old boy as well as the eighteen-year-old girl, something for the conservative Christian, and something for the wannabe punk rocker. When it comes down to ordering individual titles, knowing what your collection currently offers the community and what is circulating well within the collection along with professional reviews will help you decide if a particular title may work well within your current collection.

Relying on professional reviews is the best way to build your collections. Most library journals review children and teen materials. Some review titles for all ages, such as *Kirkus Review, Publisher's Weekly, Booklist,* and *Library Journal.* Other journals focus specifically on children and teen materials, such as *School Library Journal, Library Media Connections,* and *Voices of Youth Advocates.* While the reviews may be anywhere from 150–300 words, each library journal has criteria for their reviewers to follow. Whether it is rating scales, review styles, or the amount of critical analysis within a review, each journal has something different to offer readers. For example, *Booklist* reviews only recommended titles. You will not find any negative reviews within the pages of it. *School Library Journal* and *Library Media Connections* make their focus for school media specialists. While this does not mean that public librarians will not find value in the reviews, it does mean that the reviewers think about the material in terms of school media centers rather than public libraries. *Kirkus Reviews* is known for its book critiques no matter whether the reviews are positive or negative. Most reviewers from these journals are professional librarians who are paid a minimal amount, sometimes in the form of books. Their experiences in the field make them particularly valuable as reviewers for a library-oriented journal. When ordering materials, look for reviews that are more than a synopsis. Depending on the type of material, you may want to know specific information about it. For example, a graphic novel review should discuss the art as well as the writing. Most book jobbers (i.e., Baker & Taylor, Ingram, Brodart) include reviews in their online ordering system, which gives librarians the wonderful ability to read multiple reviews of the same title in one place. Remember that although reviewers are asked to fairly evaluate material, one journal's reviewer may give a title a starred review while another may give it a negative review. Such opposing reviews, depending on how they are written, may give a librarian enough information to decide if a title would fit well within the collection.

Once a library has materials within its collection, library staff must manage them. Collection management is the maintaining of a collection through the organization of said collection and the deselection of older, possibly outdated titles. Teen departments can be organized in many different ways, depending on the philosophy of the library. For the most part, teen book collections typically are broken down into fiction and nonfiction. Depending on the library and its shelving arrangements, these materials could be shelved separately in their own space or interfiled with either the adult or children's materials. There are advocates of both arrangements. When I began working at my library, the teen collection was interfiled with the adult collection with the exception of the paperback fiction. Many libraries that shelve multiple age ranges together are smaller libraries with less space for separation. At my library, the argument for the nonfiction interfiling was that it allowed teens working on homework assignments to find the material all in one location rather than having to go to multiple places in the library. The problem with this arrangement is that the recreational nonfiction titles get lost within the shelves of the adult nonfiction. This was the case with my library.

The first thing I did as the teen librarian was to advocate for a separate space for the books. The fiction hardback titles were hidden within the thousands of adult titles, so no teen was finding them and adults were not reading them either. With the separate space, the books flourished and we were able to discover what our community readers were reading. Beyond the move signaling that the teens were valuable partners of the library, the separation actually protected the library from potential complaints. Mixing materials for various age groups, such as teens and adults, opens the library up to potentially uncomfortable situations for both the library user and the librarian. Who wants to deal with the parent who is upset that her twelve-year-old checked out a boys' love (homosexual relationship manga written for a female audience) graphic novel meant for adults because it was with all of the other graphic novels? No one does. That is an unfortunate possibility when teens' materials are interfiled with adult materials or children's materials.

There is another public library shelving concept that has been floating around lately that breaks a teen collection down into a younger teen and an older teen collection. The argument for this arrangement is that the development that occurs between the ages of twelve and eighteen is drastic and the experiences within those six years have a wide range of issues. The materials written for this age range highlight those developmental and other experiences making older teen titles not appropriate for younger teens. This arrangement could be said to follow the many children's departments that break out the beginning readers and early chapter books from the harder ones. However, the children's arrangement is about the ability to read and comprehend the material, while the teens' arrangement is not. Instead, the separation is about the emotional development and experiences of the teen. There will be twelve year olds who act more mature than most eighteen-year-olds as well as naïve eighteen-year-olds. Libraries see them all the time.

There are two main dangers in making a collection with this type of arrangement. The first is the message the library sends to the older teen who wants to read the younger teen material. These are the "baby" books, the childish books, the books they should have already outgrown. Every year at my library, a freshman class comes in with a homework book assignment. The novel has to be at least 250 pages, the author has to be American and alive, and most important, they may not be young adult books: "You are too old for those books now." The examples of what not to get are J. K. Rowling's *Harry Potter* series, R. L. Stine, Christopher Pike, and Lurlene Mc-Daniel. For years I have written the teacher, had parents talk to the teacher, and even removed the teen label from books to try to advocate for her students the power of YA literature. In the end, the teens wind up hearing about great teen novels from me and take back to school James Patterson, Stephen King, and a few other accessible adult titles. (Although, one year the teacher did accept *Looking for Alaska* by John Green, from the spine of which a teen had removed the teen label.) The message is the same flipped for the mature twelve-year-old, who will see that the Ellen Hopkins books are not for her—that she is not old enough to handle what is contained within the pages. What about the young teen who has been sexually abused? Should she not read about a character who fought against her abuser like in *When She Hollers* by Cynthia Voigt?

The other danger is the intellectual freedom issue. How does a library determine what is for younger teens versus older teens? Is it what the publisher states? A grade five through nine gets shelved in younger teen, and a grade ten and higher gets shelved in older teen? What if the publisher says it is for ages twelve and up? Would the library buy a copy for both collections? Probably not. Most likely those titles would end up in the younger teen collection only. What about the titles that the publisher does not put a rating on? How do you decide? Do you look at reviews? What would make you decide that it would fit in older teen versus younger teen—if the review mentioned sex, drugs, or abuse or used foul language? These are some of the questions that build up the slippery slope. This is exactly why the ALA has a firm position on labeling and rating systems. Breaking down the age ranges is a form of a labeling and ratings system. This interpretation of the Library Bill of Rights states:

> Labels on library materials may be viewpoint-neutral directional aids designed to save the time of users, or they may be attempts to prejudice or discourage users or restrict their access to materials. . . . Prejudicial labels are designed to restrict access, based on a value judgment that the content, language, or themes of the material, or the background or views of the creator(s) of the material, render it inappropriate or offensive for all or certain groups of users. The prejudicial label is used to warn, discourage, or prohibit users or certain groups of users from accessing the material.[17]

In a public library setting, if space allows, the best bet is to have separate teen fiction, graphic novel, and nonfiction collections. This delineates the teen collections clearly from the rest of the library collections. It allows teenagers to be a recognized part of the library and sends the message to teenage patrons that teenagers are wanted at the library.

Self-censorship is censorship that comes from within the library staff—whether it comes from the collection development librarian, the programming librarian, the cataloging department, or the circulation department—each self-censor steps away from the policies of the library and the staff members take it upon themselves to censor. This occurs when a staff member has an ethical dilemma and, instead of following the workplace's ethical values, follows her own personal ones. It also can stem from the fear of challenges.

Self-censorship can take on many different faces. It can be from the librarian who rationalizes that the library does not need the novelty book on the best-seller list for fear of a challenge—even though the library's policy is to purchase all best sellers—because it happens to be called *Go the F**k to Sleep.* That same librarian may also decide that the library does not need to purchase O. J. Simpson's *If I Did It*, not for fear of a challenge, but because of the librarian's view of tastefulness. It can be a school media specialist who does not purchase a sexually charged but age-appropriate title like *Boy Toy*[18] for his high school library for fear of a challenge. It can be a blanket decision to not include gay and lesbian fiction in a collection. Do not assume that the self-censoring librarian only censors controversial topics that could possibly upset the conservative community. It can be a librarian who refuses to purchase sex education books published by a Christian publisher or a children's book that explains dinosaurs in terms of creationism. This type of collection censoring happens without people knowing about it. It is important that, when librarians notice occurrences, they speak up about it.

Beyond collection development censoring by the purchasing librarian, self-censoring can occur in the cataloging department when material is postponed from being processed or even hidden in desk drawers. It can happen when a cataloger decides that a topic should only be in the adult collection when a book was purchased for a teen collection. This was a challenge I had to deal with early on in my career. The books in question were nonfiction titles on self-mutilation. It required meetings of the teen librarians, the managers, and finally a meeting facilitated by the managers with the teen and cataloging staff. Again, it was an ethical dilemma from the viewpoint of the cataloging librarian of trying to protect the teens and the viewpoint of the teen staff to provide current and necessary resources for teens.

Self-censoring can occur within the programming staff as well. The fear of complaints can draw people away from ever hosting controversial programs such as new age or unexplained phenomena programs. Self-censoring can occur after a program has happened by choosing never to host it again. For example, a teens' Anti–Valentine's Day party drew complaints that the library was making fun of the holiday. Another example is a history program based on the *You Wouldn't Want to Be* book series. The presenter no longer chooses books that have any religious undertones because of questions being asked in her *You Wouldn't Want to Be on the Mayflower* program. Is it wrong in these cases to self-censor because it was the programming librarian being uncomfortable with the questions asked of her? Not necessarily, but backing away from a program because of a fear of complaints it may draw is wrong—especially when the program would have impact on teens' lives, such as a sex education workshop taught by Planned Parenthood. Also, when teen involvement is in tandem with teen programming, the teen librarians are being seen as intellectual freedom role models. If teenagers see their role model backing down from a potential complaint before it occurs, they may be less likely to step up to the plate when it is their turn to protect intellectual freedom.

Self-censoring is dangerous ground no matter what type of censoring occurs. For a thorough exploration on the topic and a survey, see *School Library Journal's* article "A Dirty Little Secret."[19] We must as protectors of intellectual freedom check our own ethical dilemmas at the door of the library.

NOTES

1. Beverley Becker, "Before the Censor Comes: Essential Preparation," in *Intellectual Freedom Manual*, 6th ed., American Library Association Office for Intellectual Freedom (Chicago: ALA, 2002), 331–46.

2. "Glendale Public Library Collection Development Statement," Glendale Public Library, last modified April 27, 2007, accessed February 18, 2012, www.glendaleaz.com/Library/documents/collection_development.pdf.

3. "Number of Challenges by Year, Reason, Initiator & Institution (1990–2010) | American Library Association," American Library Association, accessed February 18, 2012, www.ala.org/advocacy/banned/frequentlychallenged/challengesbytype.

4. "Plainview School Media Center Policies," DeKalb County Board of Education, last modified January 18, 2007, accessed February 18, 2012, www.dekalbk12.org/plainview/School%20Library%20Policy%20and%20Procedure%20Manual2.pdf.

5. "Adair County R-I Library Media Center Handbook," Adair County R-I School District, last modified February 2, 2005, accessed February 18, 2012, http://novinger.k12.mo.us/libraryhandbook.pdf.

6. Becker, "Before the Censor Comes," 331.

7. Becker, "Before the Censor Comes," 338–39.

8. Becker, "Before the Censor Comes," 340.

9. Catherine Lord, *Defending Access with Confidence: A Practical Workshop on Intellectual Freedom* (Chicago: Public Library Association, 2005), 67.

10. Ibid., 68.

11. "Sample Request for Reconsideration of Library Resources." American Library Association, accessed February 18, 2012, www.ala.org/advocacy/banned/challengeslibrarymaterials/copingwithchallenges/samplereconsideration.

12. ALA Office for Intellectual Freedom, *Intellectual Freedom Manual*, 7th ed. (Chicago: ALA, 2006), 345.

13. "Bill of Rights Transcript Text," National Archives and Records Administration, accessed February 21, 2012, www.archives.gov/exhibits/charters/bill_of_rights_transcript.html.

14. Lord, *Defending Access with Confidence*, 65.

15. Ibid., 77.

16. Ibid., 87.

17. "Labeling and Rating Systems." American Library Association, accessed October 18, 2012, www.ala.org/advocacy/intfreedom/librarybill/interpretations/labelingrating.

18. Debra Lau Whelan, "A Dirty Little Secret," *School Library Journal* 55.2 (2009): 26–30.

19. Ibid.

WHAT TO DO WHEN A CHALLENGE HAPPENS TO YOU

Kelly Tyler

AS YA LIBRARIANS working in public and school libraries, we are charged with selecting the best materials for young adults within a limited budget. Each individual purchase reflects the care and thought we put into our collection, so it is easy to feel as if a challenge is a personal attack on our professional abilities and judgment. To take a more positive approach, think of a challenge as an opportunity for you, as a YA librarian, to advocate for teens. A library is one of the only places where teens can explore controversial issues, and a challenge represents a chance for you to defend teenagers' right to have access to a wide variety of materials on any given subject. According to "Free Access to Libraries for Minors":

> Librarians and library governing bodies have a public and professional obligation to ensure that all members of the community they serve have free, equal, and equitable access to the entire range of library resources regardless of content, approach, format, or amount of detail. This principle of library service applies equally to all users, minors as well as adults.[1]

Complainants may not know why YA librarians select materials that offend some visitors. During the course of a conversation spurred by a challenge, it is our job to explain the principles behind what we do in a way that reduces the likelihood of the challenge advancing to the next stage in the reconsideration process. As YA librarians, we should let parents and concerned citizens know that we are receptive to their concerns and welcome their feedback but that we also care about privacy and access to information for the teenagers we serve.

Libraries receive challenges because we are doing our job by representing diverse viewpoints, including those that some may find provocative and sometimes offensive. Librarians select materials from a variety of viewpoints to protect the First Amendment, so we must respect that members of the public also have a First Amendment right to express disagreement with how the library does its business. Each member of the public has a fundamental right to question the activities of a governmental body and a right to due process. This is, in fact, a central tenet of the U.S. Constitution.

Receiving a challenge from concerned parents means that engaged adults are trying to help the library best serve the needs of the youth in the community. For librarians, it is an opportunity to express appreciation for this concern and explain the library's position on intellectual freedom for youth and why we believe in including diverse viewpoints.

TYPES OF CHALLENGES

A challenge is an attempt to remove or restrict materials from a curriculum or the library due to an objection by an individual or group. The Intellectual Freedom Committee (IFC) of the Office for Intellectual Freedom (OIF) has defined five types of challenges:[2]

1. Expression of concern: An inquiry that has judgmental overtones.
2. Oral complaint: An oral challenge to the presence and/ or appropriateness of the material in question.
3. Written complaint: A formal, written complaint filed with the institution (library, school, etc.), challenging the presence and/or appropriateness of specific material.
4. Public attack: A publicly disseminated statement challenging the value of the material, presenting to the media and/or others outside the institutional organization in order to gain public support for further action.

5. Censorship: A change in the access status of material, based on the content of the work and made by a governing authority or its representatives. Such changes include exclusion, restriction, removal, or age/grade level changes.

OIF has been collecting data about banned books since 1990, although for each challenge that is reported to them, as many as four or five go unreported.[3] Statistics gathered by OIF show that parents challenge materials more than any other group and that challenges happen most frequently in schools, school libraries, and public libraries, in that order.[4] Most challenges are due to concerns about sexually explicit content, offensive language, or an item's suitability for a particular age group.

Sixty-six percent of the ten most frequently challenged authors from 2001 to 2010 have been YA authors. If adult authors commonly taught in school are included, the percentage soars to 80 percent. This puts the issue squarely in the laps of YA and school librarians.

There is a long historical record of attempts to censor and suppress opinions from all political viewpoints. The hard work of librarians, teachers, parents, students, and other concerned citizens has helped ensure that most challenges are ultimately unsuccessful.[5]

RECEIVING A CHALLENGE

What do you do when you receive a challenge? How can you feel prepared for the issues and feelings that may arise when you have a discussion with a complainant?

It is easy to feel caught off guard by a complaint. Kristin Pekoll, YA librarian at Wisconsin's West Bend Community Memorial Library, says that a 2009 challenge battle waged in the media took her completely by surprise. In her case, a local family objected to a list of books on the YA part of the library website. The list, titled "Over the Rainbow," featured gay, lesbian, bisexual, and transgender fiction and nonfiction books owned by the library. "I didn't even think of these books as being controversial," says Pekoll. "I was really surprised that it happened and that it was about a website. I didn't think that it would happen to me. I didn't think that it would happen at our library." Sara Douglas, a librarian serving five through twelve at a parochial school, says she knew she was likely to receive a complaint at some point but that when it did happen it was "similar to getting a shot. Just because you know it is coming doesn't mean that you're not still a little shocked when you feel the needle pierce your skin."

The OIF has a list of commonly challenged authors and other statistics that can help you prepare for common challenges. But what happens when someone asks you a question about why you have a biography of Pol Pot? How will you prepare yourself for the possibility that any book in your collection, any content on your website, or any posting your social media accounts could be challenged?

KNOW POLICIES AND PROCEDURES

It is difficult to react to an unexpected question or concern if you are not already familiar with your library's materials selection policy and its procedure for complaints. Complainants may be confused, angry, concerned, frustrated, or all of the above. Your goal should be to quickly and simply address their concerns in a knowledgeable manner. You should be prepared to clearly explain your library's materials selection policy, the philosophy of intellectual freedom, particularly as it applies to teens, and the process for challenging library materials. Douglas, the parochial school librarian, points out that complainants will be able to tell if you are unorganized. Preparing yourself ahead of challenges, "will help you keep a calm, professional demeanor throughout this stressful time."

Kimberly Hirsh, a school librarian working at a rural middle school, adds that knowing your service population can help you justify the inclusion of an item in your collection. She recommends that you "know the library's policies" and that if your library does not have a collection development policy "you should create one and make sure that those who will be enforcing it have given it their stamp of approval." She recommends the OIF Workbook for Selection Policy Writing for helpful information on creating policies and dealing with challenges (www.ala.org/bbooks/challengedmaterials/ preparation/workbook-selection-policy-writing).

KEEP EMOTIONS IN CHECK

When a library user takes issue with materials in the YA collection, it is easy to get defensive, particularly when attacks take on a personal tone. In Pekoll's case, the challenge became directed at her professional abilities and responsibilities. "It really felt personal. I felt I had done something wrong." You may also feel a sense of anxiety. That's the word Hirsh used to describe how she felt when the parent of a sixth grader objected to the language in a book in the collection. Douglas says she felt "raw panic" when her director informed her of a complaint about *Nick and Norah's Infinite Playlist.*

Challenges are likely to make you feel angry or upset. After all, you selected these materials to best serve the young adult population that visits your library. As professional YA librarians, we think about issues of diversity, intellectual freedom, teen identity, and popular appeal all the time, so it is easy to get offended when we feel that our professional judgment is being called into question.

Even if you are angry, it is important to receive any complaint calmly. You are not only a YA librarian, but a representative of your library too. As the first contact for the complainant, keeping your emotions in check can prevent the escalation of a challenge. Even if you will refer the complaint to your supervisor or another administrator within the library, you still have to engage with the complainant and you are the library's first line of defense.

Douglas knew that the parent who raised a challenge did not want her at a meeting because he wanted to say bad things about her. She says that she had to keep her emotions in check to make sure the meeting ran smoothly. "Keeping calm and taking the time to think through what you are about to say before you say it will help the process get resolved without escalating it with hurt feelings and raised voices."

HEAR AND RESPECT THE CONCERN

No matter the source or the content of the complaint, listen to the concern with respect. Most complaints come from parents[6] who may not know that librarians carefully consider their purchases and are guided by the principles of intellectual freedom. Engage complainants and ensure that they know you are carefully listening to their concerns. By using active listening skills and being respectful, you have a good chance of keeping a challenge at the lowest level possible.

Be sympathetic, but do not agree that the material is objectionable. As you are receiving the complaint for the first time—before you have not had time to review the material and develop an appropriate response—try to keep the discussion focused on the broader issues rather than on the merits of the specific item being challenged. In many cases, a parent or other complainant may be satisfied after being heard and having the selection policy and intellectual and academic freedom philosophies thoughtfully explained. Emphasize why the library places these guiding principles above the personal opinions of any single person or group. Make sure that the complainant understands that the items in the YA area are selected for teens of all ages and that parents are ultimately responsible for helping their teens select the material that best meets the needs of their family. It also may be prudent to point out that, while some material may not be of interest to all teens, minors and adults alike are afforded the same free and unrestricted access to materials under the First Amendment. Parents and guardians, not libraries and other governing bodies, are responsible for determining a minor's level of access to library materials.

In Douglas's case, the parent at her parochial school was concerned about material in *Nick and Norah's Infinite Playlist* that was "not Christian." Douglas knew that the main issue was the use of offensive language. Because she had read the book in advance of the meeting she had with the parents and the school's head, she was able to carefully and thoughtfully explain how the language was used in the context of the book and to describe the positive moral values addressed in the book. She also used the opportunity to explain that, because the library is used by both middle school students and older teens, she uses red dots to indicate high-school-level titles. However, these dots are for information only and she does not restrict students' access to books. After receiving this information, the parents "lost steam," says Douglas, and dropped the challenge.

If complainants wish to take the next step in the complaint process, inform them that the library cannot address anonymous concerns and that to proceed they must submit a request for reconsideration. Make sure that they are given a copy of the selection materials policy and a copy of the complaint procedure. When they complete the request for reconsideration, make sure they are told who will be contacting them and when they can expect to hear from the library.

GETTING SUPPORT

Though most people who challenge library materials may be satisfied after a discussion with a librarian who thoughtfully and thoroughly explains library selection policy, some may still wish to fill out a reconsideration form. Once you receive a formal complaint of this nature, defined as a written complaint by the OIF, where do you turn? There is an abundance of support within and outside the library profession to assist you and your staff in your journey.

OIF has a wealth of support on its website (www.ala.org/bbooks) including tips for effective communication, advice on how to deal with a challenge, statistics about challenges, and suggested ways to prepare for a challenge hearing. They also provide information to help you prepare yourself in advance of a challenge by writing and publicizing policies to make the public aware of the guiding principles behind the purchase of materials for teens in your library. OIF offers free, confidential assistance to librarians and educators addressing challenges (oif@ala.org or 800-545-2433 x. 4220).

The YALSA Intellectual Freedom Interest Group maintains an electronic mailing list (yalsaintellectualfreedom-ig@ala.org) for the discussion and dissemination of information about issues relevant to intellectual freedom for teens in school and public libraries. The interest group is a support system for YA librarians dealing with pressures to diminish the rights of teens and also serves as the liaison between YALSA and the ALA IFC.

The YALSA and American Association of School Librarians electronic mailing lists are also rich sources of assistance and support. Douglas says that after she heard about the challenge to *Nick and Norah's Infinite Playlist*, the first thing she did was get on her electronic mailing lists to see if others had dealt with a challenge to this particular book. She calls "the great community of librarians" "super supportive," as she immediately received "countless e-mails of advice and support. They definitely helped me feel less alone in the situation."

IFC is charged with safeguarding the rights of all library users and works closely with the OIF to address issues of intellectual freedom and censorship as they relate to libraries. The IFC identifies emerging social, political, and technological trends that may require resolutions, policies, or guidelines to assist librarians as they fight efforts to curb intellectual freedom.

Check to see if there is an intellectual freedom committee of your state library association. They should be aware of any state regulations or laws that may apply to you. They may have other resources available to assist you during the challenge process.

The National Coalition Against Censorship (NCAC) (www.ncac .org) is a coalition of fifty not-for-profit organizations (including ALA) dedicated to addressing censorship concerns. NCAC has addressed issues including academic freedom; lesbian, gay, bisexual, transgender, and queer (LGBTQ) content; self-censorship; artistic expression; and youth self-expression. The coalition has a First Amendment in Schools Toolkit as well as information about advocacy and censorship in a variety of settings.

FTRF, an affiliate of ALA (www.ala.org/groups/affiliates/relat edgroups/freedomtoreadfoundation), is a First Amendment legal defense organization. FTRF aids individuals and groups that are engaged in the legal defense of First Amendment rights, and it directly participates in litigation around issues of freedom of speech and freedom of the press.

The American Civil Liberties Union (ACLU) does much toward protecting civil liberties in the digital age. They work against Internet censorship, including elimination of filters installed on school computers. Other helpful ACLU resources for YA librarians include information on freedom of speech for students and LGBTQ youth rights. ACLU also provides information about current legislation and landmark decisions on First Amendment rights.

SLATE stands for Support for Learning and Teaching of English. It is the grassroots advocacy network for the National Council of Teachers of English (NCTE). Each year the group gives its Intellectual Freedom Award to individuals, groups, or institutions that have advanced the cause of intellectual freedom. NCTE has an anticensorship center where teachers and librarians can find advice on handling a complaint about materials used in the classroom, guidelines for dealing with challenges to nonprint materials, and defenses for commonly challenged books.

REVIEWING A WRITTEN COMPLAINT

A written complaint should be reviewed as soon as possible. Your library's policy should indicate who is responsible for reviewing the complaint. During the reconsideration process, the material that is being challenged should not be removed or restricted in any way.

Depending on the size and structure of your library, it could be an individual or a committee that will determine whether or not the challenged material should be retained according to the collection development policy. A committee may include the librarian who selected the item, the librarian who serves the target audience for the material, and the librarian with administrative responsibility for the department. The policy should include specific guidelines for the individual or committee responsible for making a recommendation. Though this may vary by library, in many cases committee members will be charged with:

1. reviewing the reconsideration of materials procedure
2. reviewing the library's materials selection policy, the criteria for the selection for the material, and any policies the library has about access to materials
3. reading or viewing the challenged materials in their entirety
4. reading the request for reconsideration to determine the reason for the challenge and the action that is being requested

5. checking critical reviews to determine the opinion of experts and critics
6. determining whether these materials are readily available for purchase and are in demand within in the community served by the library and investigating other local or similar libraries and their holdings of the material in question
7. meeting to discuss the challenge
8. making a defensible recommendation based on the findings

Whatever recommendation has been made, the complainant should be notified of the decision. The library's written response should address the concern, inform the complainant of the decision and the rationale behind it, and let the complainant know how to appeal the decision.

If the complainant is not happy with the decision of the library, the next step is typically an appeal to the governing board of the library, as defined in your library's complaint procedure policy.

During the reconsideration process, it is important to refrain from discouraging members of the public from exercising their First Amendment rights to speak up about their objections. Being respectful and courteous in accepting constructive criticism from the public honors the democratic process.

WRITING A RATIONALE

What Is a Rationale?

Educators use rationales to justify their use of materials in the classroom. Rationales contain information that explains why materials are selected for use in the curriculum and can be helpful if a parent has questions. They can also be used during the reconsideration process to demonstrate the merits of materials that have been challenged.

Why Write a Rationale?

OIF recommends that school librarians develop rationales for the use of required materials to help parents understand what is being used in the classroom and why. Distribution of rationales along with your school's educational goals and materials selection policy can be a proactive way to preempt potential complaints from parents about materials in the library collection.

In a public library setting, rationales may also be a helpful tool for defending a challenge during the reconsideration process. Rationales in a public library setting will help library users understand why an item was originally purchased for the collection and how it fits into an overall vision of YA services.

Content of a Rationale

The content of a rationale may vary but should minimally contain these items:

- ▶ a complete bibliographic citation
- ▶ a description of the intended audience
- ▶ a brief summary of the work
- ▶ a list of references for critical reviews of the work

Depending on the challenge and your situation, it may also be helpful to include this information:

- ▶ aspects of style, texture, tone, and theme that may be problematic for students and ways that the teacher plans to address these issues
- ▶ student outcomes that are expected if the teaching objectives are met
- ▶ a list of alternative books that parents can select for their own child if they do not wish to have them read the selected text
- ▶ a list of awards received by the work
- ▶ an explanation of how the work meets the criteria specified in library's selection policy or, at a school, the curriculum
- ▶ information about the availability of the work within other libraries and community retail outlets used by members of the community

Using a Rationale during the Reconsideration Process

As a YA librarian, you may or may not be involved in making a recommendation about an item that has been challenged in your collection. If you are not the person who makes the recommendation or you are not serving on the committee that makes the recommendation, writing a rationale is a good way to make sure that those on the committee have all the necessary information to make an informed decision.

If you are serving on a committee tasked with reviewing a request for reconsideration, a rationale can help you prepare for your discussion with colleagues and help you defend the item if you believe the library should retain it in the collection.

As mentioned before, rationales can also be used to give information to parents, administrators, and other colleagues in advance of a challenge or during the challenge process to address expected or expressed complaints. Offering concrete evidence of why the material has value will make it easier for you or your administration to mount a defense.

CONDUCTING A CHALLENGE HEARING

Challenges only occasionally reach the point of requiring a hearing in front of the library's governing body. If a challenge does reach this point, you should continue to rely upon your library's procedures and policies. Planning ahead, staying organized, and keeping the process open and transparent to the public will ensure that your library has the best chance of retaining the material without restriction.

Before the Hearing

Your library's complaint and reconsideration procedure should indicate who will be making the decision after the hearing. Before the hearing begins, make sure that all members of the governing body are familiar with the selection policy and have been given time to review the challenged material in its entirety. Make sure the administrative head of the body is aware of the procedures that should be followed and knows that the meeting will be open to the public and that public comment will be invited.

Make sure that the complainant is made aware of the recommendation that the library staff is making to the governing body in advance of the hearing. Coordinate with the complainant to ensure that the hearing is planned at a time when she is able to attend.

Make sure that the meeting space is large enough to accommodate everyone who may attend to prevent last minute changes in location. Announce the hearing in advance so there is ample opportunity to make the public aware of what will be discussed and any decisions made by library personnel prior to the hearing in front of the governing board. Make sure that it is clear that the meeting is open to the public. Make copies of your policies and procedures available for review by the public in advance of the meeting. Contact news outlets to get coverage by your local press, and create a press release for your library's website.

Make arrangements to tape the hearing and record minutes that can be publicly distributed. Consider designating seating so that those favoring removal are on one side of the room and those opposing removal are on the other. This will prevent one group from monopolizing the choice front seats.

Rally supporters who will advocate for your library. Contact the OIF for support. Even if they cannot send a representative, they may be able to write a letter of support to bolster your cause. You should also get support from your local community. Identify leaders in your community who are willing to speak in support of libraries and intellectual freedom. Consider getting teens involved to speak about why they support intellectual freedom and oppose having the material in question removed or restricted. Make sure that your lineup of speakers is set well in advance of the hearing and that these advocates have been given a copy of the selection policy and other helpful documents such as the Library Bill of Rights. Those selected to testify during the hearing should be reminded that they are defending the principle of intellectual freedom, not the merit of specific items.

If a representative of the library will be speaking, the OIF has a series of questions and answers that can help them prepare for the types of questions that may be asked during a hearing. The speaker should remember to respect due process, remain calm, and use good communication skills to speak broadly about the importance of intellectual freedom within the framework of the library's service to teens.

During the Hearing

As people arrive, make sure they receive a copy of your library's materials selection policy and any other supporting documentation such as the Library Bill of Rights. Attendees should also receive a statement about the hearing, detailing the chain of command for the decision-making process as well as how the materials selection responsibility is delegated to the professional staff of the library.

Make sure it is clear at the beginning of the meeting that it is a hearing and that the board in charge of making a final decision will be doing so at a later date. Speakers should be allowed to speak in the order they signed in, and each speaker should be given the same time limit. A timekeeper should be selected in advance. No speaker should speak a second time until everyone has been given an opportunity to speak once. It is important to adhere to the agenda and all the time limits.

After the Hearing

After the hearing has concluded, make any recordings and minutes available to the public and news media outlets as soon as possible. The announcement of the committee's decision should be made by the board at the next regularly scheduled meeting. The agenda should indicate that the announcement will be made, but the decision should not be released in advance of the meeting. Publicize the meeting and consider issuing a news release on the library's website.

When the board releases its decision, the policy of the library should be summarized and the board should state a reason for the decision.

In the aftermath of a hearing or of any challenge, it is a good idea to look at the policy and procedures for challenges to determine if they are up-to-date and whether they cover questions you might receive about YA materials and services, reflecting current issues and trends about complaints received at other public and school libraries. If you find that the policy could use improvement, advocate for your administrative decision makers to consider rewriting the policy.

NOTES

1. "Free Access to Libraries for Minors," American Library Association, last modified 2008, accessed March 26, 2012, www.ala.org/advocacy/intfreedom/librarybill/interpretations/freeaccesslibraries.

2. "Challenges to Library Materials," American Library Association, accessed March 26, 2012, www.ala.org/advocacy/banned/challengeslibrarymaterials.

3. "100 Most Frequently Challenged Books by Decade," American Library Association, accessed March 26, 2012, www.ala.org/advocacy/banned/frequentlychallenged/challengedbydecade.

4. "Number of Challenges by Year, Reason, Initiator & Institution (1990–2010)," American Library Association, last modified 2010, accessed March 26, 2012, www.ala.org/advocacy/banned/frequentlychallenged/challengesbytype.

5. "About Banned Challenged Books," American Library Association, accessed March 26, 2012, www.ala.org/advocacy/banned/aboutbannedbooks.

6. "Number of Challenges by Year, Reason, Initiator & Institution (1990–2010)," American Library Association, last modified 2010, March 26, 2012, www.ala.org/advocacy/banned/frequentlychallenged/challengesbytype.

INTELLECTUAL FREEDOM

Programming and Marketing

Karen Jensen

NTELLECTUAL FREEDOM IS an important concept that librarians working with teens should embrace and fight for. Teen lives are fraught with a variety of challenges, and teens want—and need—authentic reads that reflect their lives and inform them of the real world that they live in. Teen fiction spans a wide array of ages, topics, and ideals, and some authors choose to realistically depict teen challenges in their fiction. Our job is to stand up for teens' right to read it and help make sure it is there for them to find and connect with.

My conviction for intellectual freedom was solidified when I myself became one of the challenged. It all began with a display during Banned Books Week. Using the manual supplied by ALA, I chose a variety of challenged books, wrapped them in brown paper, and identified why they had been challenged or banned because of what was once the cover. The library I was working at had a massive slat wall that provided space for large displays that made quite a visual impact. Although we got a lot of compliments on our display and had some discussions about the importance of intellectual freedom, one patron was offended that we were telling children and teens to read these books. Of course, we were not telling them to read or not read them. What we were trying to do was help them understand that they should have the right to make that decision for themselves. In this particular instance the patron complained all the way up the administrative chain until she made it to the public library board. Thankfully, the board understood and supported the concept of intellectual freedom, and the display stood its ground. But from that moment on, I understood clearly: censorship is a real threat.

Intellectual freedom is an important concept, a value that the library must educate the public about. Library marketing means more than just promoting our services and collections; it means promoting our values and helping our communities (patrons) understand what we bring to them. Marketing intellectual freedom means that we help our communities understand the value of access to a wide variety of thoughts and ideals and encourage them to speak up for the library as an important part of personal intellectual growth and democracy. Marketing intellectual freedom to teens lets them know that we value them and promise to uphold their personal rights, and that we respect their reading interests as we endeavor to provide materials, programs, and services that meet their needs.

BUILDING A FOUNDATION FOR INTELLECTUAL FREEDOM

In order to promote and market intellectual freedom, libraries should have a variety of elements in place:

1. a clearly and concisely written intellectual freedom policy that makes it clear to staff and patrons that the library supports the concept of intellectual freedom
2. a clearly and concisely written material selection policy that outlines the libraries goals, audience, and purpose in its collection development processes
3. a clearly and concisely written materials challenge form that allows patrons the opportunity to express their concerns and guides staff and patrons in navigating any concerns (One main component of any good material challenge is the requirement that a patron read the entire written work before being able to challenge said work. One cannot judge the value of a work by picking out "offensive" words and phrases, which does not create a holistic picture of the work's style or message.)

4. staff training that makes sure staff understand the value of intellectual freedom and equips them with the tools and phrases they need to deal with a hostile patron on the front lines

With these elements in place, as discussed earlier in this work, your library has set a strong foundation to move forward. Now you can create displays and programming with the sure knowledge that if you have a challenge, you have the tools you need in place to address them with a sure footing.

And be assured, patrons can and will challenge anything and everything, from a title on your shelf to the listing of a book on a bookmark and, yes, even the concept of intellectual freedom and Banned Books Week displays. There are those factions who truly do not understand the concept of intellectual freedom, which is part of the reason that we must promote it. Our goal is to help our communities understand that we endorse nothing in our collections, but we endorse a reader's right to access them. In short, if we have something in our collections that offends them, then we have done our jobs because we are representing a variety of viewpoints not a singular one.

MARKETING INTELLECTUAL FREEDOM

Marketing is everything you do to get your customers involved with your product. Marketing involves an exchange of information and is usually focused on building a relationship.[1] Your goal is to create a relationship with your teens and help them understand a concept and become participants. Here, you are trying to get teens to value your library as an important service provider that is willing to take a stand on an important issue—intellectual freedom. Your message is simple: because we value you and we value your rights, we work to provide what you need and want. By asserting the value of intellectual freedom to your teens, you are de facto asserting the importance of the library in the lives of teens. There is no other place where teens can come and get unfettered access to these materials.

Marketing is a process, and programming can be a meaningful part of that process. Programming is a way of making your library and your message visible in the community. It increases awareness. It gets teens involved. Your audience members cannot know and understand your message unless you deliver it to them multiple times in multiple formats. Every teen is different and speaks a different language. Some teens will respond to a display while others may need a video. Each different format that you use to deliver your message increases the number of teens that you will reach.

Take a moment and think of the way movies are currently marketed: there are trailers, movie posters, web campaigns, viral marketing campaigns, and memorabilia, for example. They approach the market in various formats, as should we. A simple sign or bookmark is not enough; they blend in with all of the other signs and bookmarks that populate our libraries.

Think also of large corporations that have made marketing a value part of their brand, like Nike. They do not just sell a shoe; they are selling a lifestyle. Their message of "Just Do It" is very clear: whatever it is you want to do, get out there and do it with everything that you have, and of course a Nike shoe is just the thing you need to make that happen. That is our goal with marketing intellectual freedom; we are marketing a value and showing how the library helps the community maintain this vital freedom. As the Nike shoe is to embracing your athletic dreams, the library is to embracing your intellectual freedom. One cannot exist without the other. That is the message we are trying to convey to our audience.

Many teens (many patrons in general) are not even aware of the fact that books get challenged. If we do not work to raise awareness, it will be easier for books to simply disappear off of the shelves. Teens cannot exercise and defend a right unless they understand what that right is and the threats that are posed to it. By doing displays and programming to raise awareness about intellectual freedom, you are equipping your teens to be aware, informed, and able to fight for their rights.

When discussing the topic of intellectual freedom, I always use the Bible as a prime example. Many people who object to materials do so from a religious point of view and in the interest of protecting a cultural standard morality that they often base on Biblical viewpoints.

However, the Bible is historically one of the most challenged books in history. The Bible has been challenged for violence and sexuality, for example. In addition, if you study the history of the Bible, you see that there were great attempts made to keep it in a language that prevented access among the common people. This gave the church all the power to control the masses. This is one of the reasons why access to information is so important; it allows individuals the opportunity to read and study and determine for themselves. When Martin Luther translated the Bible into a language that everyone could understand, he was giving them individual power and, in a way, standing up against a form of censorship as well as promoting intellectual, and in this case spiritual, freedom to the people.

ESSENTIAL MARKETING STEPS

As with any form of marketing, there are three essential steps you must take:

1. Define your message.
2. Define your audience.
3. Get the message to your audience.

Define your Message

Our message is this: intellectual freedom is important and cannot exist without your library. Your goal is to communicate this value to teens and help teens understand the various threats against that value. This means you must help them define the concepts of intellectual freedom, censorship, book banning, and a challenge. Your job is to help them understand the value in being able to access a wide variety of materials and choose for themselves whether or not a book is right for them. Marketing a value is harder than marketing a product or service. It is not a one-time event. Teens cannot come to your program on Monday after school, make a craft, and move on with newfound knowledge of the value. It is an ongoing marketing challenge that requires librarians to be diligent in making sure our message is understood.

Define your Audience

If you work with teens, you should have a good grasp of your audience. The teenage years are important developmental milestones; it is that time when teenagers move from dependence to independence and are trying to define who they are and what they believe. The teen years are important years to teach and embrace the concept of intellectual freedom. They are also difficult years, as parents still have legal rights and responsibilities to their teens and the library must honor those in very specific ways. So, although it is important that we provide access to materials, it is also important that we respect the role of the parent. How that happens will depend upon your library's policies and procedures and is the primary reason that clearly outlined policies are vital.

But what else do we know about teens? Teens, like every other group of people, are living very diverse lives. Despite what many adults want to think, teens are having sex, living in abusive homes, and navigating a reality that some parents may not want their own teens to read about. As library branch manager Josh Westbrook said, "Kids are living stories every day that we wouldn't let them read."[2] These teens need to be able to read stories that reflect the realities in their lives.

For additional information to help you understand your audience, check out resources like Ypulse, the Frontline series on the teenage brain on PBS (available online), and the 40 Developmental Assets developed by the Search Institute. Understanding who your audience is will help you understand how best to reach them.

Get the Message to Your Audience

There is a variety of ways that you can raise awareness about intellectual freedom issues from the simple (displays) to the more complex (programming). The idea is to get library patrons thinking about some important censorship issues: Who gets to declare items inappropriate? Where do we draw the line? A common belief around the idea of censorship is that the books that we find inappropriate will be banned or challenged, yet history proves that is not the case. While some may object to the use of wizardry in the Harry Potter series, others write about the gospel according to Harry Potter (*The Gospel According to Harry Potter* by Connie Neal). The truth is, no two readers respond to a work of fiction in the same way and every reader has the right to decide for themselves—this is the heart of intellectual freedom and the message that we must convey to our teens.

A prime opportunity to raise awareness in your community about intellectual freedom issues is the Banned Books Week that takes place in September of each year. This is a time when libraries across the country come together, and there is power in a message that takes place on a scale of this magnitude. This should not be the only time that you raise intellectual freedom awareness with your community, but this is a time that you should not ignore.

GET YOUR AUDIENCE INVOLVED

The most effective marketing campaigns are those that get your audience involved, if at all possible. Do not just tell them that intellectual freedom is important; make them tell you. As teens create slogans, displays, and artwork that defend the concept, they are more likely to buy into and internalize the concept. When Mountain Dew creates a campaign that asks their drinkers to name their next flavor of Dew, they are creating this type of ownership. That is what we want to try to do by getting teens involved in our intellectual freedom programming and marketing.

For example, if I were going to do my Banned Book display today, I would put the books on display wrapped in brown paper bags with a brief multiple choice quiz giving teens the opportunity to guess why that title was banned. This draws your audience in and asks them to participate. The best way to get teens involved is to get them thinking and creating. By giving teens the opportunity to be creative, you are asking them to think through what their message is. Here they internalize the concepts and become defenders of the value. By moving from the passive to the active, teens become your marketing voice, send the message for you, and become advocates for your library.

Sarah Amazing, teen librarian at Warren-Trumbull County (Ohio) Public Library, sees this transformation take place each year during Banned Book Week:

> Every September in the teen space of our library we have a display of banned books, complete with lists of those frequently challenged & giveaways such as bookmarks & pins that declare "I read banned books." It's become a tradition of sorts that at that month's Teen Advisory Board meeting, I go through the list announced by ALA of the previous year's challenged, giving the reasons provided, & have the books available to the teens. They usually all disappear into their bags to be checked-out. We then have a discussion about the week & why it's so important that information not be censored, & now it's just amazing to watch one of them defend a book when someone questions it. When I purchased "Banned Books: Challenging Our Freedom to Read" by Robert P. Doyle last year, they poured [sic] over it for hours, excited every time a banned book was one they had already read.
>
> As a teen librarian, I take a special interest in intellectual freedom, since books published for this age group make up the bulk of the list nearly every year. If teaching about anti-censorship begins anywhere, I truly believe that it's with teens.

PROGRAMMING IDEAS THAT GET TEENS INVOLVED

You want your teens thinking about, writing about, and creating around the concept of intellectual freedom and censorship. You want them to move beyond a passive observance and really get involved in understanding the concept and fighting for their rights as readers and information consumers. To do that, it is important not only to put visuals in place for teens to see, but to set out programs and times where we can genuinely engage in discussing the issues with our teens (see figure 4.1). The teen years are full of intelligence and passion; it is important that we get them talking about the issues that affect their lives. Your goals are to get teens involved in the discussion, make a powerful statement, and make sure that everyone walks away understanding that the freedom to read is an essential freedom that they want to defend.

FIGURE 4.1

MARKETING AND PROGRAMMING RESOURCES FOR BANNED BOOKS WEEK

There is a wealth of valuable information online ready for you to use in your marketing and programming for Banned Books Week (BBW). The sites below all contain valuable information for you from lists of books that have been banned/challenged to detailed program outlines and ideas. The ALA website and American Booksellers Foundation, in particular, provide a good look at the various titles that have been banned/challenged and the reasons why.

The Basic ALA Guide: www.ala.org/bbooks

Banned Book Week Website: www.bannedbooksweek.org/

ALA's List of BBW display ideas: www.ala.org/ala/issuesadvocacy/ banned/bannedbooksweek/ideasandresource/display_ideas/ index.cfm

The American Booksellers Foundation list of display ideas: www .abffe.org/bbw-display.htm

The American Booksellers Foundation list of books challenged/ banned and the reasons why: www.abffe.com/bbw-booklist.htm

Random House teacher's guide to censorship: www.randomhouse .com/highschool/resources/guides3/censorship.html

Teach Hub 12 Banned Books Week Classroom Activities: www .teachhub.com/banned-book-week-activities

Chris Crutcher BBW Posters (designed by author Karen Jensen): www.chriscrutcher.com/extras.html

Teen Librarian Toolbox Facebook page: www.facebook.com/media/ set/?set=a.267944093231661.84565.222736761085728

Teen Librarian Toolbox Blog on BBW: www.teenlibrariantoolbox .com/search/label/Banned%20Books%20Week

Here are some ideas that do just that:

- Set up an attention-grabbing display. Holly Thompson Frilot had a simple and effective way to communicate the importance of intellectual freedom. She put up a display of empty shelves, declaring that all the books had been banned, as shared on the Facebook wall for my blog, Teen Librarian Toolbox (TLT) (see figure 4.2).
- Tie what is currently popular with teens to the concept of intellectual freedom. For example, take a popular novel, like the *Hunger Games* by Suzanne Collins, and discuss how the Capitol controls the access to information by controlling what people see on the TV feeds and how they fight this censorship by finding ways to tap into the feed.
- Want to get a teen to read a book? Tell them they cannot. As librarian and freelance writer Elizabeth Warkentin points out, telling someone—especially a teen—that they cannot do something is one of the best motivators to get them to do it. Nobody likes to be told that they cannot do something, and that is especially true for teen boys. So put up a display of books telling them they cannot read them and watch them fly off of the shelves. Even better, get them reading and discussing the books.[3]
- Ask teens to design Banned Books Week/Freedom to Read posters as part of a contest. You can put them on display throughout your library and share them electronically on your library web page and various social media sites.
- The Washington-Centerville (Ohio) Public Library got teens involved in thinking about censorship by putting together a simple contest. The contest sheet included the covers of several challenged/banned titles and asked teens if they could guess why the books were censored. They also did a book display to promote the contest. They put the message out there in interactive ways and via multiple formats, increasing its power.
- Have teens create new book covers for their favorite banned book. Ask them to convey the importance of the book and why it is being challenged. You can use these book covers to

decorate your teen area and share them online to send your message. Teens can also create posters in general about the concept of censorship. Have teens create bookmarks, posters, and more defending their right to read in general or to read particular book titles. This is a great way to tap into teens' creativity and multimedia expertise.

▶ Hold a town hall type meeting to discuss the issue of intellectual freedom.

▶ Hold a mock trial. Again, this is a way to get teens thinking about censorship in general and the specific merits of individual works. You can also put a character from a book on trial. Or put a banned author on trial. Teens can do some prep for the trial by writing to the author in question, or you can have a teen pretend to be the author in a program. You could also do this as a modern day talk show. If you have the creative ability, turn your event into an interactive murder mystery where teens get involved in the mystery: "Who killed the book?"

▶ Create a book trailer for a banned book or a PSA against censorship in general. There is a variety of easy tools teens can use to make short videos that can easily be shared. Naomi Bates has some information on how to create book trailers on her blog, and there is also some information about making book trailers on TLT.

▶ Simply choose to read and have a book discussion about a banned book. Or have a community read. Before you read the work, tell teens why the book has been challenged or banned and then ask them afterward what they thought. Oftentimes parts of a book are taken out of context, and reading the book can help teens understand that people need to read a complete work before they can understand the author's vision or message.

▶ Have people read out loud from banned and challenged books. Simply set up an open stage area with chairs and refreshments, and schedule readers throughout the day. Teens can come in and sit at their leisure and listen to live readings from the very books the censors want silenced.

▶ In addition to reading challenged books, you can read and discuss works about censorship such as *The Day They Came* to *Arrest the Book* by Nat Hentoff, *Fahrenheit 451* by Ray Bradbury, or *1984* by George Orwell.

▶ The Matched series by Ally Condi and the Delirium series by Lauren Oliver both involve a future world in which a majority of the written texts we now take for granted are banned. Both of these series are a great choice for reading and discussing with your teens patrons. In the Matched series, there is a list of 100 authorized poems and art pieces that are authorized. Have teens see if they can come up with a list of 100 titles that they all agree on that would be authorized. Any programming that involves these two series would be an excellent inclusion to your Banned Books Week programming.

▶ If you have access to local or popular authors, tap into these resources and ask them to write or do a library visit to discuss the topic.

▶ Have teens read Judy Blume's book on censorship, *Places I Never Meant to Be: Original Stories by Censored Writers*, or ask them to visit Blume's website (http://judyblume.com/cen sorship.php) where she talks about censorship, then talk to teens about it. You can even ask teens to write their own short stories about censorship.

▶ Share intellectual freedom news with your teens. Chris Crutcher, an intellectual freedom advocate and an often challenged author, works hard alongside Kelly Miner Halls to raise awareness about intellectual freedom issues and to encourage teens and librarians to participate in Banned Books Week. He documents ways that teens have challenged censors on his website (www.chriscrutcher.com/teens-can -stop-censors.html). You will want to visit this site and share these resources with your teens.

▶ Look for other examples to share. For example, in 2012 teens rose to the challenge in Arizona when the Mexican-American studies program was declared illegal and many of the books were boxed up and removed from the classrooms. Students took up protests, made signs, spoke at board meetings, and so on to help fight their cause. Debbie Reese documents this at her website, American Indians in Children's Literature.[4]

▶ If you have the means, provide a free e-book for download, making sure that the title chosen is somehow relevant to the topic by either being a banned book itself or being a book on the topic of censorship such as *Fahrenheit 451*. Or have a contest where the prize is an e-reader preloaded with a certain number of challenged/banned books.

▶ If you have a teen advisory board, enlist them to stand outside your library for a period of time with masking tape over their mouths, holding a large sign that shows a banned book cover and the reason the book was banned or challenged.

▶ Let the chalk do the talking for you and have a program where teens use sidewalk chalk to write about Banned Books Week outside your library. This will create a strong visual as patrons walk into the library.

▶ Host a mixer and invite participants to come dressed up as characters from their favorite banned books. Cosplay is a type of event where participants dress up as characters. *Cosplay* is in fact short for "costume play." A variety of libraries have had events where they have mixers and invite teens. You can even create a type of Comic Con inspired event that focuses on intellectual freedom.

▶ Fanart and Fanfiction (also known as fanfic) are highly popular on the Internet and allow teens to get creative with and respond to their favorite literature. These are tremendous tools that you can utilize to get your teens involved with discussing censorship. For example, a previous Teen Read Week activity that many participated in called the Book Quote Celebration[5] would be easily adaptable to a Banned Books Week event. Here teens are invited to make, or take, pictures inspired by their favorite works and incorporate meaningful quotes into the picture. Fanfiction.net is one of the largest online storehouses of fanfiction. In addition, there is a website devoted entirely to Harry Potter fanfiction that you can explore for examples at www.harrypotterfanfiction.com.

▶ You can also set up book battles and have teens campaign for their favorite banned books. Teens should be encouraged to create pins (kits can be bought cheaply at craft stores and provided): posters, banners, and more for their favorite titles. You can set up a debate or allow teens to come up to a podium and make speeches in defense of their favorite titles. Or you can do a simpler book battle version where you post a battle a day on your social media site and allow teens to vote for a winner. The winner moves on to the next round until one book is left standing. Or you can do book battles by genre categories and have a variety of winners, one for each genre.

▶ Many fiction fans use crafting to create personal memorabilia inspired by their favorite books, and this would be a simple program to plan with your teens. You can do things like marble magnets, bottle cap crafts, and dog tags (again, all available at most craft stores) that incorporate teens' favorite banned books. To make all of these crafts, teens can use words from magazines, scrapbook papers, and more to create a saying or statement that relates to the work. This same concept can be used to decoupage almost any item, including memory boxes ("Don't let the freedom to read become a memory"), candle holders ("Fahrenheit 451 is the temperature at which books burn"), and picture frames. (See figure 4.2.)

▶ Murals are a great way to display artwork created by teens on the topic of censorship and intellectual freedom. You can create unique display places by using corkboard, strings with clips, or even clipboards. For example, see Putting the "Teen" in Your Teen Space at www.teenlibrariantoolbox .com/2012/02/putting-teen-in-your-teen-space.html.

▶ You can provide specific pages for teens to complete, such as comic book cells to create comic book strips or graphic novel page layouts, and ask teens to create comics and graphic novels about censorship. Or simply allow them to be creative and display it.

FIGURE 4.2

CRAFT IDEAS AND RESOURCES FOR BANNED BOOKS WEEK

Craft programs are a great way to get teens involved with the discussion on intellectual freedom and allow them creative ways to express themselves. In addition, when you do book-inspired crafts, you are connecting teens to literature. In the most basic form, you can simply get teens to create book-inspired art freestyle by having them make posters, bookmarks, and so on. Some teens, however, need more direction. These activities are easily adapted to be book inspired. You can also provide teens with quotes on intellectual freedom for them to incorporate into their craft and art projects.

Bottle Cap Jewelry

Pull double duty by discussing intellectual freedom and hosting environmental crafts with these bottle cap crafts. Simply use banned/challenged book covers or words that relate to intellectual freedom in your project.

www.squidoo.com/bottlecap-necklace-pendants

Bookmarks

Create bookmarks to hold your place in your favorite banned book.

www.teenlibrariantoolbox.com/2011/08/tpib-pageturners-save-my -spot.html

Book Page Crafts

Online there is a variety of crafts made from actual book pages. Make flowers, butterflies, birds, and leaves out of the pages of discarded books. Teens could come together in a program to make these elements, and you can put together a fabulous display about the power of words. Imagine creating a tree with leaves made from book pages surrounded by flowers, birds, and flowers made from book pages with a statement like "What would the world be like without books?"

http://rustic-crafts.com/?p=5180

(continued)

(continued from previous page)

Marble Magnets

Make mini-magnets inspired by favorite books or including words that speak to the freedom to read.

http://thefrugalgirls.com/2010/10/marble-magnets-tutorial.html

Meme All the Shirts

Tap into the very popular meme trend and allow teens to create their own intellectual freedom–inspired meme shirts.

www.teenlibrariantoolbox.com/2012/07/tpib-meme-all-shirts
-heather-booth.html

Peel Away Book Quotes

Use either your favorite quotes from banned/challenged books or quotes about intellectual freedom to make amazing book quote canvases.

www.libraryasincubatorproject.org/?tag=the-mortal-instruments

EXPAND YOUR MESSAGE WITH SOCIAL MEDIA

As you plan your approach, consider using social media tools to expand your message and get teens involved. As a part of my blog, I did an activity that engaged teens and tapped into their use of social media called "Tweet for FREADOM." The concept was simple; teens were invited to tweet a slogan defending their right to read as part of a contest.

The entries submitted all addressed the idea that censorship is bad for society. This contest tied together two important elements: the idea of intellectual freedom and teens' use of social media. What you end up having is teens creating slogans for Banned Books Week and sharing them online with all of their peers. Your audience becomes your messenger. Here are some other ideas for engaging teens through social media:

- Post a book a day and have teens guess the reason why the book was challenged/banned. *Or give the reason and have them guess the book. You can make it multiple choice if you want.*
- Make a simple contest sheet *where* you remove the titles from books and have teens guess what the book is and match the reason it is banned/challenged. You can upload the contest sheet so teens can download it and turn it in. You can also make them available in your teen area for pick up.
- Tap into teens' creativity and ask them to design book covers or posters for Banned Books Week. During that week have a drop-in workshop. Share the images electronically to raise awareness.
- Have an online book discussion of a Banned Books Week title.
- Share a YouTube clip a day of a movie that was made from a challenged or banned book.
- Share a variety of online resources by "pushing" links through your feed. For example, in this YouTube clip John Green discusses the fact that he is *not* a pornographer: www.youtube.com/watch?v=fHMPtYvZ8tM.
- Find online resources like this and share them electronically with your patrons. Try to find one post a day to share

for the week with your patrons and invite them to respond. Here is one to get you started from Open Road Media: www .openroadmedia.com/blog/2011–09–24/Banned-Books -Week.aspx.

▶ Share articles and online discussions about teen fiction and whether or not it is too dark with your teens and get them discussing it. What do they think about the fiction they read?

▶ Ask teens to write a Twitter feed describing a world in which reading was not allowed.

▶ Share a quote a day about Banned Books Week. Find quotes at www.ala.org/template.cfm?section=bbwlinks&template=/ contentmanagement/contentdisplay.cfm&contentid=87403.

▶ Every day share a link to an author that has been chal- lenged/banned.

▶ Set up a Banned Books Week website and invite teens to write letters to their favorite banned and challenged authors. You can also include spaces for their created artwork. By making this site open to the public, some of the authors may choose to respond to your teens and validate their efforts. I can think of no more empowering message for teens than to get this kind of feedback from their favorite authors.

▶ *Take one day and make your pages go completely silent. That is what would happen if censors had their way.*

Many of the ideas mentioned above are taken from TLT. Check the site for new ideas. You can get additional programming ideas by searching the web or visiting ALA's website.

PROMOTING INTELLECTUAL FREEDOM YEAR-ROUND

When you are thinking of doing displays, contests, and more, think of ways you can bring intellectual freedom issues into the equation. Remember, this does not have to be a once-a-year event. The truth is, book challenges pop up at all times in all places, which means we should be promoting the message about intellectual freedom at all times and in all places.

Stay informed, and keep your eyes open for any book challenges that pop up. Hopefully you are subscribed to professional forums such as the Yalsa-bk electronic mailing list so that you can keep your fingers on the pulse of current book news. When book challenges pop up, share the information with your community. Yes, it may not necessarily impact them locally, but fighting for intellectual freedom rights affects us all. Keep your community members informed about book events like these through your various social media outlets and get them involved in the discussion. Make sure to share these types of events with library staff as well (and do not forget your library board). These are teachable moments that libraries can use to reinforce their message regarding intellectual freedom.

TALKING WITH STAFF

It is a good idea to have some type of weekly communication with staff, such as an e-mail update or wiki, where you can keep staff informed of best sellers, current events, trends in pop culture, and so on. This is also a good tool to keep your staff thinking about intellectual freedom issues and keep them informed of any current challenges. You can also provide your staff with "what if" scenarios to help them think about the issues involved and how they will respond.

Working with teens is a nice, fuzzy, intellectually gray area. They are still not technically adults and do not have the various legal rights that adults have, but they are definitely on the road to adulthood. In fact, the teenage years are very formative identity wise, which makes the access to information that much more important. Many teens are wrestling with sexuality, sexual identity, and personal religious beliefs—these and others are hot-button issues that many adults, both parents and library staff, are uncomfortable talking about. Many of us understand intellectual freedom and assume that our staff does as well, but that is not always the case.

Most libraries hire a detail of nonprofessional staff to take on tasks such as paging, working the circulation desk, and even doing basic technical processing duties. These staff members need to be trained to understand the concept of intellectual freedom and be advocates as well. They need to be trained about your library's policy and procedures, and you need to do role-playing situations where the staff is taught how to interact with patrons in these types of situations. It is important to remember that these patrons are coming to you with strong convictions and these can be difficult situations to deal with. It is imperative that part of our customer service training include knowing what to say and how to say it in these types of situations.

Several times in my career as a YA librarian I have had staff members come to me from the technical services department and tell me that they thought I should not put a book in the collection. You would not think it would happen, but it does. In one instance, a book was challenged—although not formally—by a staff member who had stumbled across a racy scene while flipping through the pages. It is a key factor to note that, in all of these instances, the staff member had never read the entire work being questioned. In most of these cases the titles in question were graphic novels and the staff members in question formed their opinions simply by flipping through the pages and catching a picture that bothered them. Make no mistake, graphic novels can pose a unique challenge because of the visual element. In addition, not all graphic novels are written for a teen audience, making policy and selection a very delicate issue. My response was always succinct and straightforward: we have a material challenge process in place and everyone, including staff, must follow it.

In these types of instances, it is imperative that you acculturate all staff to the mission of the library—the overall mission of the library as an institution and your library's specific mission in your community. Training and advocacy help get all of your staff on the same page.

RESPECTING TEENS' CHOICES

Fundamentally, when we are promoting intellectual freedom we are promoting the rights of teens to decide what is right for them. Some teens may respond quite favorably to a work while other teens may be offended. Depending on their backgrounds, they may even be unnerved by some materials and choose not to finish them. That is a choice we must support. I have read many a comment over the years regarding someone who has struggled with body issues not being able to read *Wintergirls* by Laurie Halse Anderson because it has the intensity to take one to a place of vivid memories.

Jacqui Milliern, a youth services librarian from Mitchell Community (Indiana) Library, tells the following story regarding respecting teen choices:

> On Friday I held an art program for grades K–12 (I work at a rural library, so we had a manageable 39 registrants). As per usual, at the beginning of the program, I asked the participants to separate into two groups. Usually those two groups are junior high and high school, but this time I separated two groups based on whether the attendees wanted their art to include artful nudes or to be censored. Every teen chose to be in the censored group! To me, this is an example of patrons choosing Intellectual Freedom.
>
> I tell every teen that I interact with in the reader's advisory interview that it is okay not to like a book and even not to finish it. If it is not the right book for the right reader it can do incredible damage in the same way that the right book in the right hands can make all the difference in positive ways. Teens need to understand that part of intellectual freedom is the freedom to decide that a book is not the right book for them.

THE FIGHT FOR TEEN LITERATURE

In the past few years teen, or YA, literature has been under tremendous amounts of scrutiny in the press. Some readers suggest that teen literature is too dark.[6] They tend to focus on certain parts of teen literature, particularly the current trends in paranormal romance and dystopian fiction, and paint a broad category with a fine-tip paint brush. They also fail to understand that if you take a moment to peel back the layers of some of the darkness, the underlying message is that you can fight against oppressive governments, rise above difficult family situations, and find laughter in the midst of difficult situations.

Teen literature speaks to teens because it is authentic and reflects where they are in their development and their worldview. While it may be easy for adults to stand on the outside and decide what they think teens should read, think, and feel, teens need to be able to access literature that speaks to the heart of who they are and where they are in their lives. This is the crux of intellectual freedom. A teen growing up in one home may have an entirely different point of view and lifetime of experiences than a teen growing up in another. Both teens need to have access to literature that reflects their values and experiences. And they need to have access to literature that allows them to experience a life different than their own. This is how we develop compassion and a more reflective, and accurate, worldview. This is one of the primary goals of literature—to open up the door to the world and help teens take the baby steps necessary to understand the reality that is this world.

This is where things like book discussion groups, multicultural programming, and readers' advisory services come into play in promoting intellectual freedom. We need to help teens gain access to a variety of worldviews and experiences, to open their minds to the struggles around them, and to help them process that information. When a book that is potentially challenging comes along, which would help our patrons more: inviting parents and teens to read and discuss the book or pull it off of the shelves and pretend that those controversial things do not happen in our world? One of the greatest gifts adults can give teens is the opportunity to discuss their thoughts and feelings and really let them be heard.

READER'S RIGHTS

At the end of the day, our goal in promoting intellectual freedom is this: we want our patrons to understand that we offer a diverse collection and that not everything in our collection may be right for them, but it is right for someone. The most basic thing we can do is to put up signage expressing every reader's basic rights: the right to read what they want and to let others do the same.

Intellectual freedom is an ongoing issue in the library world, and teen services can often be an uncomfortable area for those who are not familiar with the whys and hows of intellectual freedom. Part of our jobs as teen services librarians is to advocate for their rights, which means we must be advocates for intellectual freedom both in our libraries and in our communities. With the proper policies and training in place, you can put on your advocacy hat and use the above scenarios to keep the topic in the forefront of your library goals. With everyone informed and on the same page, you and your library are in a better position because you will already have staff and community support on your side.

NOTES

1. "Introduction to Marketing," Marshall School of Business University of Southern California, Lars Perner, Ph.D, last modified 2008, accessed April 16, 2014, www.consumerpsychologist.com/marketing_introduction.html.

2. Joni Richards Bodart, *Radical Reads 2: Working with the Newest Edgy Titles for Teens*, Scarecrow Press (Maryland: Scarecrow Press, 2009), xxii.

3. "Banned books help hook boys on reading," *Toronto Star*, Elizabeth Warkenkin, last modified February 27, 2012, accessed April 16, 2014, www.thestar.com/life/parent/2012/02/27/banned_books_help_hook_boys_on_reading.html.

4. "AICL Coverage of Arizona Law that resulted in shut down of Mexican American Studies Program and Banning of Books," American Indians in Children's Literature, last modified January 24, 2012, accessed April 16, 2014, http://americanindiansinchildrensliterature.blogspot.com/2012/01/aicl-coverage-of-arizona-law-that.html.

5. "Teen Read Week 2011: Book Quotation Celebration," Teen Librarian Toolbox, last modified July 18, 2011, accessed April 16, 2014, http://teenlibrariantoolbox.blogspot.com/2011/07/teen-read-week-2011-book-quotation.html.

6. "Banned Books Week: Teen Fiction Is…," Teen Librarian Toolbox, last modified July 21, 2011, accessed April 16, 2014, http://teenlibrariantoolbox.blogspot.com/2011/07/banned-books-week-teen-fiction-is.html.

ACCESS IN THE DIGITAL WORLD

Linda Braun

DO YOU REMEMBER the summer of 2006 when the Deleting Online Predators Act (DOPA) was the focus of debate in the United States Congress? A focal point of DOPA was that youth need to be protected from predators in online social spaces. To provide that protection, Congress debated a federal law that would require schools and libraries that received e-rate funding to prohibit minors' access to sites that required registration. If DOPA had passed, it would have meant that sites from Amazon to Facebook to You-Tube to course management systems like Moodle would have been inaccessible to young people of all ages in many schools and public libraries.

It was an interesting debate, as it demonstrated the struggle so many have with understanding the capabilities of the web and social networking and balancing those with the desire to help young people be safe online. It also demonstrated that the issues related to access in the digital world are broad and that making good decisions about teen access to materials in this expansive space requires a knowledge of technology, a knowledge of adolescent development, and a knowledge of how to educate young adults to guarantee they have the critical thinking and decision-making skills needed to use virtual materials in smart and safe ways.

Although DOPA did not make its way out of Congress and into law, it was just one of several bills at the federal level that have attempted, by limiting access, to protect young people from dangerous situations in the digital world. State legislatures have also worked to create and pass laws that limit youth access to digital materials. Laws can seem like a good way to keep children and teens safe, but in the fast-moving digital world, it is nearly impossible to pass a law that is fair and that realizes the unintended and long-term consequences of limiting access.

No one could have imagined when the Mosaic web browser launched about 20 years ago[1] what access to the web would allow teens to accomplish. The web 2.0 world of social media was not even a glimmer in most of our eyes all that time ago. It is the ever-expanding nature of digital access that creates great challenges for those working with teens. The battles for access continue, and that means that librarians need to stay on the forefront of what is happening legally (in the federal, state, and local arenas) and continue to advocate for access to digital content by teens in schools and libraries.

WHY TEENS NEED DIGITAL ACCESS

For many librarians working with teens it is second nature to support teen access to print materials. These are the materials that most librarians grew up with. (The youngest, newest librarians are the first who grew up with technology as a part of their day-to-day lives. We have not yet seen librarians in the field who have used social media throughout their lives.) Library school conversations cover the importance of intellectual freedom and access to a wide range of print materials. It is fairly new, however, for library school classes to focus on the importance of access to digital materials for teens. It is also new for faculty to have a full understanding of what digital materials are and of the role of library staff in providing access to these materials.

Some readers of this chapter may even wonder themselves, "Why should teens have access to digital content?" Some may think that, because it is impossible to evaluate and select every digital resource that a teen might access, digital access should be limited. Yet, in order to support teens successfully, limitations on access to content often end up limiting a teen's skills and knowledge of how to be safe and secure in online spaces.

THE DIGITAL WILD WEST

The wide-open sometimes frontier-like nature of the digital world is exactly why teens need access in schools and libraries. Do we want teens to go out on that frontier without having skills to determine what is safe to take part in online? Do we want teens to be pioneers without understanding how to critically think and problem solve while on the frontier? Do we want teens to be uncomfortable talking about what life is like as a pioneer and what they need help with? The answer is of course, no. Access to digital content in the library gives teens the chance to learn, practice, and discuss.

One way that libraries are giving teens this opportunity is through learning labs. YouMedia at the Chicago Public Library was one of the first spaces of this type.[2] In the YouMedia learning lab environment, teens are given opportunities to create and collaborate on content where adults are available to help and advise. Adults assist teens with the technology. Adults also talk with teens about a host of topics related to using technology successfully.

Imagine that teens are working on a video that they plan to post on Facebook and YouTube. As the teens work on the video, the librarian can talk with them about copyright and about the positives and negatives of posting content in social spaces. These conversations are what is required to give teens an understanding of how to behave online and how to react if something unfortunate happens to them when in online space.

Keep in mind as well that sites like YouTube contain an extraordinary amount of educational content of value to teens. The federal government is on YouTube, the Smithsonian Museum and National Geographic post videos on YouTube, zoos, libraries, foundations, and a host of other institutions have made educational videos available through this site. If schools and libraries block this content, then they are truly keeping teens away from learning opportunities. That is not the purpose of course, but it is a consequence.

Think too of the teens who need access to information that they might not otherwise be able to access except in virtual spaces. A teen who has a question about sexual identity or a health-related issue may not have an adult she trusts enough to ask questions. If that adult is not available, then a website like Go Ask Alice, from the Columbia University Alice! Health Promotion Department, could be just what the teen needs to get accurate information. What about a teen who has a question about a religion and does not feel comfortable asking his parents or friends because the question is about a religion other than the one they practice? A site like Belief.net could be exactly what the teen needs. If these sites are blocked because of filters, then what is a teen to do?

DISPELLING THE MYTHS

One thing I have discovered is that there is a great deal of misunderstanding about what laws actually require of schools and libraries when it comes to blocking access to resources. In some instances schools and libraries, because they receive e-rate funding and because of CIPA, assume that all social sites have to be blocked because of that regulation. However, this is not the truth. The rules of CIPA[3] speak to blocking access to visual images deemed "obscene," "child pornography," or "harmful to minors." CIPA does not specifically say, as some assume, that schools and libraries have to block YouTube. As Tina Barshegian points out in her excellent article "Dispelling Myths About Blocked Websites in Schools." If the technology fails us and filters something appropriate and useful, and if teachers in their professional judgment think it's appropriate, they should be able to show it. Teachers need to impose their professional judgment on materials that are available to their students."[4]

It is easy for a school or library to say that it will block all social sites. That way no one has to spend time looking at sites, considering their positive implications, talking with colleagues and teens, and so on. It is a one-step answer. However, easy is not effective in making sure teens have what they need to grow up successfully.

Instead of the one-fell-swoop approach, each resource needs to be evaluated individually. In some instances, even if a resource is known to have materials that could include inappropriate content (e.g., YouTube), it still may need to be made available, with the knowledge that adults have to help teens learn to navigate these resources successfully. Do we say to teens, no, you cannot go to the newsstand because there are magazines that might not be appropriate to you? No. We help teens understand which magazines are appropriate and which are not. Do we say to teens, you cannot go to Barnes and Noble because some of the materials on the shelves are not appropriate to you? No. We teach teens how to be smart about what they spend time looking at while in a bookstore. I realize that in a bookstore and newsstand the perception that people—customers and staff members—will see what teens are looking at will keep teens from spending time with inappropriate materials. However, that is not always true. There are plenty of places in Barnes and Noble where a teen could sit with material that some might think is inappropriate. We need to give teens the skills they need to make good choices and then trust that we have done the job well.

There are also myths surrounding what teens do and do not understand when it comes to digital materials. Some assume that teens are unaware of how to be safe while online, and while teens take risks online—as they do in many areas of life—young adults do know a good deal about privacy and safety in the digital world. A 2011 report from the Pew Internet and American Life Project that focused on teen kindness and cruelty in social sites found that " most teens are cognizant of their online privacy and have made choices to try to protect it."[5] While teens might make mistakes about who they interact with online or how they behave, that does not mean they are not aware of the potential negative consequences of their choices. Librarians and teachers need to continue to help teens understand what the potential is for dangerous consequences to their online actions. This has to be done through access, not by banning access.

BEING A DIGITAL ACCESS ADVOCATE

Library staff needs to understand the value of teen access to digital materials and then be ready to advocate for that access. That requires being able to articulate to different audiences the why of teen digital access. It takes more than simply stating that teens like technology. The real key is articulating how libraries can help teens to be better users of technology by providing access.

It is likely that when advocating for digital access for teens that you will need to talk to different audiences. You might have to talk with administrators, colleagues, town officials, business people, and more. You may have the same basic message from audience to audience, but the way you present it will likely have to vary. Before you advocate for digital access to a particular person or group make sure to do your homework. Find out what concerns your audience has and be able to address them from the teen advocate and library perspective. Is a concern that teens accessing YouTube will find inappropriate content? If that is the case, then make sure to talk about the benefits of YouTube for teens and how using YouTube gives teens the chance to engage in conversation with adults about the ins and outs of social media and being safe online. Explain that by teaching how to use YouTube in a safe environment you are limiting the possibility that teens will happen upon inappropriate materials when on their own.

If someone is concerned about teens sharing too much information on Facebook or other social networking sites or being targeted by pedophiles on social sites, be ready to talk about the privacy features of social sites, what the real statistics are on teens and privacy and safety with social media, and how teens need to learn from adults about social sites and how that means providing access within safe spaces. Discuss how giving teens the chance to interact with the library on a Facebook page can include instruction on privacy settings and safe use. Explain how using Facebook in a class can allow for discussion of what to do if someone unknown tries to befriend a teen via the social site.

When you advocate for teen access to digital materials, make sure to have strong examples of positive uses of social sites and other web and mobile technologies at the ready. The following provides some good places to start.

Google Docs

As a web-based collaboration tool, Google Docs is a perfect example of the value of social technologies in teen lives. Yet, I have had librarians tell me that they are not able to use Google Docs with teens because of concerns over privacy. There is no way to be 100 percent safe in virtual environments; however, the basic features of Google Docs makes it easy to set up a file so that either the teen creating the document is the only one who has access or the teen can carefully select who to share the document with to collaboratively develop content. Making decisions about document ownership is one thing teens need to practice. Not using Docs means less opportunity to gain that practice.

A group of teens using Google Docs can brainstorm plans for a library program that they are helping to organize. The document can be easily updated by the teens involved, and they can even work on it synchronously when in separate locations. The librarian working with the teens can add comments and suggestions to the document and keep up on the group's progress. The teens can determine if others should be included as editors or viewers to the document along the way. Perhaps they will want to give other teens the chance to see what is being planned but do not want the other teens to have editing capabilities. They can make that decision and proceed accordingly.

Pinterest

Bulletin boards came to the web in full force with Pinterest. Two primary ways that librarians and educators use Pinterest is to post booklists in visual form and to find and publish images of classroom and program ideas. For example, a Pinterest board titled Teen Programming in Libraries includes images of everything from Japanese cupcakes to masking tape paintings—all as a way to inspire teen librarians. When it comes to teens, using Pinterest can be a useful tool when collecting information for school projects. Teens can collect images on a Pinterest Board and focus specifically on Creative Commons licensed images. Each image always links back to the original source, making citing of resources easily accomplished. Teens can also create boards from the perspective of a figure in history or a book character. For example, what would Napoleon put on a Pinterest board? Or, what would Katniss's board include?

As teens create the boards, they have to critically think about what content gets their message across. Since teens can include annotations for the images they pin, they need to think about the best ways to describe their images for a particular purpose and audience. Commenting is also possible on Pinterest. This means that teens can learn about having successful conversations online.

Twitter

For several years, there was debate on the topic of whether or not teens used Twitter. Then in early 2012 it was reported that teens were using Twitter, partly as a way to keep their lives and postings private just among friends.[6] With its 140-character limiting format, Twitter provides great opportunities to teens for considering audience and message and determining the best way to get a point across. Keeping writing short is hard, and writing in 140 characters can be very difficult. What words need to be shortened? What abbreviations need to be used? How do you make sure that what you say will be understood by readers? That all takes skill and critical thinking.

Twitter has proven to be a successful way to have conversations about books, homework, and other topics with teens. Teens who have trouble being able to articulate their ideas in long-form writing have the chance to get started with those ideas in the Twitter framework. Teens can also communicate with adults, from experts to celebrities, via Twitter. If a teen wants to ask a favorite musician a question, chances are she will be able to do that on Twitter. If the teen needs to find out how to use a database at the library, chances are he can Tweet the library and ask. The technology is a tool for information and for recreation.

Teens' interest in, and awareness of, the need to keep certain content private is clear in the news reports focused on young adults using Twitter. This is an important insight worth mentioning in discussions of positive uses of technology in teen lives. It can help you to highlight teen awareness of issues related to privacy and of how to make sure that their lives are private.

Xtranormal

Xtranormal is a video creation tool that enables users to create dialogues or monologues using cartoon-style characters and sets. Creation of the videos requires making decisions about what characters and sets are the best for a particular topic and audience. Teens also write a dialogue, add special effects, music, and camera angles to help get their message across.

Teens may create Xtranormal videos that focus on book characters talking with each other about events in their stories or videos that have characters from different books talking with each other about their lives and adventures. (What would Harry Potter say to Bella?) People from current events or history discussing their lives and adventures. (What would Napoleon say to George Washington?) Students talking with each other to explain a classroom concept. (Here is what we have to do for our science projects.) And so on. Although the web-based video creation tool was not created for teens, it provides a wide array of opportunities for teens to engage in learning activities from writing to editing to storyboarding.

POLICIES AFFECTING DIGITAL ACCESS BY TEENS

Computer Use Policies

A few weeks ago I was talking with some librarians about teens and technology and was reminded of the policies libraries often implement that have unintended consequences and that work to hinder teen access to technology-based resources. One of the librarians mentioned that the teens love using her library's express computers, partly because they have fines on their library cards and therefore are unable to use the computers available for longer-term access. Other librarians in the discussion noted that their library policies were the same. While at the heart this policy is not written to keep teens away from digital content and the access they want and need, the result is just that.

Imagine a teen that does not have technology at home and her access at school is limited. The only place that might provide the full access needed is the public library. But wait; the teen has a five-dollar fine on her library card, and because the library uses library cards as a way for teens to reserve computer time, the teen is entirely without access.

It is true, in some cases, owing money or materials to the library should lead to limits on library privileges. But, those limits have to be considered within the larger picture of what the library must provide for a particular audience. For teens, the library may be the one place where it is possible to look up information on a sensitive subject. For teens, the library may be the only place to learn how to use technology tools successfully. Policies that get in the way of that are not serving teens effectively.

What can the library do? Reevaluate policies and make sure that they are still reasonable and that the ramifications of rules and policies fit the "crime." Is five dollars the level at which a customer's access should be denied? It is pretty easy to rack up a five-dollar fee on a library card, and as a result it is possible that quickly many teens will not have access to the technology. Would the punishment for the crime be better if it were 100 dollars? Sure, five dollars is five dollars, but taking away access at that level may do more harm to teens than it helps the library to get payment for overdue or lost materials.

One might wonder why—when the library is a community institution that is needed as a way to help close the digital divide—something so important to teens is used as punishment. With physical books, if there are so many fines that checkout is not possible, the book can still be read in the library. However, for many teens, access to information is unavailable because of rules that are outdated.

Device Policies

Teens are sometimes singled out when it comes to hardware access in the area of devices such as Kindles, iPads, Nooks, and so on. Libraries have policies that allow adults to check out the devices or use the devices within the library building. Children too are often allowed to use the devices in the library building. But, then there are teens. Teens are sometimes disallowed from that use. The reasoning is often based on fear that teens will not be as responsible with the device as an adult or even a child (who may be using the device under adult supervision).

However, by not providing the access to teens, libraries end up limiting a teen's ability to learn how to use new technology. Teens who do not have access to these kinds of devices in school or at home may find that the library is the only place where they can actually see how they work and gain firsthand experience. Teens also might find reading on a device a way to gain privacy when wanting to learn about certain topics. Devices might be the perfect format for reading about topics that a teen might be embarrassed about reading in public. No one will see the cover of the book the teen is reading on sex or bodies or falling in love. It can be kept completely private when using a device.

Adults, teens, and children all might break or lose a mobile device. Instead of limiting access to teens, a more positive and open approach would be to put policies in place that outline exactly what the ramifications are for anyone of any age who loses or breaks or mishandles a device. A good example of this is seen with the Portland (Maine) Public Library's circulation of Nooks to teens. On the blog post that announces teen access to these devices, specific information is provided on circulation and replacement polices. The page also specifically states who is liable for a device if loss or breakage occurs.[7] Of course, the same policies should exist for customers of all ages.

Social Media Policies

Collection development policies are used by libraries as legal documents that support the library's methods for acquiring materials. In the social and web world it is important to develop policies that support the work librarians do to guarantee teens have access to the materials that they want and need. Many schools have acceptable use policies that parents or students sign on a yearly basis and that describe how technology can and cannot be used by students. Some schools and public libraries have social media policies that outline how social tools can and cannot be used by library and educational staff. These policies may state that teachers or librarians cannot use social media at all. They may set out parameters for limited social media use. Or, the policies might open the door for teachers and librarians to connect with teens in social media spaces as a way to enhance and extend teaching, learning, information gathering, and recreational reading and materials.

Although it might seem that social media policies do not have a connection to teen digital access, they do. In the social media and social networking environment, librarians realize that it is important not to expect teens to come to them, but librarians have to go to teens. A teen might be working on a research project and have his Facebook page open at the same time. If a teen sees that the librarian in his school or public library is on Facebook, he can start a chat with her and get some answers to questions about the work he is doing.

This goes beyond homework support. A librarian may post on Twitter, Facebook, or via a YouTube video information about materials online and in print that supports a teen's informational needs on topics from sexual identity to religion to eating disorders to tax filing. This extends access to this information. When social media policies stop staff from using social media, then teens may be denied access to resources they need in order to grow up successfully.

THE LEGAL LANDSCAPE

This chapter began with mention of laws related to teen access to digital content and it ends on the same topic. Several laws (like DOPA) have been proposed in the United States Congress that work to limit access. Other laws including portions that speak to limiting access, but are not the main focus, have also been proposed. Some, like CIPA, make it through the process. Others get stalled along the way. No matter what, those working with teens in libraries must keep up with what is on the table that potentially has an impact on teen digital access. Library staff have to be ready to advocate, educate, and inform members of the community about what teens need when it comes to all aspects of the virtual world.

States have passed and proposed laws that can and do have an impact on teens and their access to digital content. These include the New York State education law on Internet safety and appropriate use (passed in 2010), which states that school districts may teach Internet safety and that the Education Commissioner will provide resources and technical support for such teaching.[8]

The New York State law opens the door for schools and libraries to give teens opportunities to learn safety by using tools that might otherwise be filtered. For example, teachers and librarians can use YouTube to teach how to be safe on YouTube. This type of law can act as a boon to access. Librarians and teachers have to seize these kinds of opportunities and use them as a way to provide access and education.

Because laws change regularly, it is not possible to provide an up-to-date rundown of what the legal status is across the United States in the area of teen digital access. However, there are tools educators and library staff can use to stay current and informed. These include:

- **OpenCongress** is a website that tracks all legislation that can be searched for up-to-date information on the status of bills in the house and the senate. The site aggregates news reports and blog postings about each bill and makes it easy to keep current on what is happening to a particular piece of legislation. Users can subscribe to bill updates via email and RSS options. The site also provides a simple to use interface for contacting representatives to inform them of your support or opposition to a bill.
- **ALA Washington Office** provides a host of resources to help librarians learn about what is going on nationally, regionally, and at the state level. Like OpenCongress, the ALA Washington Office does not focus only on teen issues or on digital issues. But, by reading the Washington Office District Dispatch Blog you will have access to information on a variety of laws proposed or on their way to passing that have an impact on teen access. By subscribing to alerts from the Washington Office's Legislative Action Center you will get news of legislative activity that you may want to respond to by contacting your representatives at the state or national level.
- **State and Regional Legislative Alerts** are often available from state and regional library association websites. In many instances these alerts are powered by Capwiz and provide information on the most recent legislation affecting libraries at

the state and national level. You can find your state's Capwiz information with the URL http://capwiz.com/ala/twolet terstateabbreviation. For example, for the North Dakota Library Association Capwiz Action Alert page you would use http://capwiz.com/ala/nd. It is possible to subscribe to action alerts and legislative updates via these sites. It is also possible to contact your state or national representatives to let them know what you think about a pending bill or issue being discussed.

▶ **YALSAblog** provides information on a variety of topics that have an impact on access to materials by teens. This includes information on pending legislation that those serving teens should know about. Intellectual freedom, advocacy, and legislation are categories on the YALSAblog that you will want to keep up with.

Do not wait to let someone else make sure teens have the access to digital content that they need. Educate yourself on the issues, talk to teens and other adults, advocate for teen access, and keep up with laws and new technology. It is your job as someone who works with teens to do these things. How else are teens going to be served as they deserve?

RESOURCES FOR LEARNING MORE AND KEEPING UP WITH TEEN DIGITAL ACCESS TOPICS

ALA Washington Office—www.ala.org/offices/wo
Beth's Blog Social Media Policy Category—www.bethkanter
.org/category/social-media-policy
Born Digital in Video—http://cyber.law.harvard.edu/
node/6385
Hack Education—http://hackeducation.com
Hanging Out, Messing Around, and Geeking Out— http://
mitpress.mit.edu/catalog/item/default
.asp?ttype=2&tid=11889
MindShift: http://mindshift.kqed.org
Open Congress—http://opencongress.org

Pew Internet and American Life Project Teens Category—
    www.pewinternet.org/topics/Teens.aspx
Teens and Social Media in Schools and Public Libraries: A
    Toolkit for Librarians and Library Workers—www.ala.org/
    yalsa/sites/ala.org.yalsa/files/content/professionaltools/
    Handouts/sn_toolkit11.pdf
YALSAblog—http://yalsa.ala.org/blog

NOTES

1. "World Wide Web," *Wikipedia*, Wikimedia Foundation, February 23, 2012, http://en.wikipedia.org/wiki/World_Wide_Web#History.

2. "YouMedia: Youth Powered 21st Century Learning: About Us," *You Media*, Chicago Public Library, February 23, 2012, http://youmediachicago.org/2-about-us/pages/2-about-us.

3. "Children's Internet Protection Act, CIPA: A Brief FAQ on Public Library Compliance," Wisconsin Department of Public Instruction, July 30, 2014, pld.dpi.wi.gov/pld_cipafaqlite.

4. Tina Barshegian, "Dispelling Myths About Blocked Websites in Schools," Mind-Shift, September 20, 2011, http://mindshift.kqed.org/2011/09/dispelling-myths-about-blocked-websites-in-schools.

5. Amanda Lenhart, Mary Madden, Aaron Smith, Kristen Purcell, Kathryn Zickuhr, and Lee Rainie. "Teens, Kindness and Cruelty on Social Network Sites. Part 3: Privacy and Safety Issues," Pew Internet and American Life Project, November 9, 2011, http://pewinternet.org/Reports/2011/Teens-and-social-media/Part-3/Private-profiles.aspx.

6. Anne Collier, "Teens Flocking to Twitter for Privacy?" Net Family News, February 6, 2012, accessed February 23, 2012, www.netfamilynews.org/?p=31220.

7. "Hey Teens, Wanna Borrow A NOOK?" Portland Public Library Teens, February 13, 2012, accessed February 23, 2012, http://pplteens.wordpress.com/2012/02/13/hey-teens-wanna-borrow-a-nook.

8. "Internet Safety," New York State Education Department, October 17, 2011, accessed February 23, 2012, www.p12.nysed.gov/technology/internet_safety.

MOST CHALLENGED YA BOOKS, 2006–2011

The Internet Girls. **Lauren Myracle.** New York: Amulet Books.
   2004. *ttyl.*
   2006. *ttfn.*
   2007. *18r, g8r.*

DESCRIPTION: *ttyl,* the first in the *Internet Girls* trilogy was the first novel written entirely in the style of instant messaging conversation. The three main characters in the series are good girls that sometimes make bad decisions. Myracle depicts high school experiences such as sex, drugs, and changing parental relationships through the girl's frank online discussions.

REASON FOR CHALLENGES: offensive language; religious viewpoint; sexually explicit; unsuited to age group

AWARDS AND MEDIA CONNECTIONS
Quick Picks for Reluctant Young Adult Readers, 2005.

REVIEWS
Booklist 100, no. 18. (May 15, 2004): 1615.
Booklist 102, no. 15. (Apr 1, 2006): 36–37.
Booklist 103, no. 14. (Mar 15, 2007): 45.
Bulletin of the Center for Children's Books 57, no. 10. (Jun 2004): 430.
Bulletin of the Center for Children's Books 59, no. 10. (Jun 2006): 463–464.
Horn Book Guide to Children's and Young Adult Books 17, no. 2. (Fall 2006): 390–402.
Horn Book Guide to Children's and Young Adult Books 18, no. 2. (Fall 2007): 361–382.
Kirkus 5. (Mar 1, 2004): 71.
Publisher's Weekly 390–402. (Mar 1, 2004): 71.

Publishers Weekly 253, no. 8. (Feb 20, 2006): 158.
Publishers Weekly 254, no. 3. (Jan 15, 2007): 54.
School Library Journal 50, no. 4. (Apr 2004): 158, 160.
School Library Journal 53, no. 6. (Jun 2007): 155.

The Story of Life on the Golden Fields, Dong Hwa Kim. New York: First Second.

2009. *The Color of Earth.*
2009. *The Color of Water.*
2009. *The Color of Heaven.*

DESCRIPTION: This manga trilogy is about a Korean teen named Ehwa and her widowed mother. As Ehwa comes of age and sees her mother falling in love again, she opens up to the possibility of love in her own life.

REASONS FOR CHALLENGES: nudity; sex education; sexually explicit; unsuited to age group

AWARDS AND MEDIA CONNECTIONS
Booklist's Top 10 Graphic Novels for Youth, 2009.
Great Graphic Novels for Teens, 2010.
Texas Library Association's Maverick Graphic Novels List, 2009.

REVIEWS
Booklist 106, no. 1 (Sep 1, 2009): 90.
Booklist 105, no. 19/20 (Jun 1–Jun 15, 2009): 64.
Bulletin of the Center for Children's Books 62, no. 10 (Jun 2009): 401–402.
Kirkus 6 (Mar 15, 2009): n/a.
Kirkus 11 (Jun 1, 2009): n/a.
Kirkus 18 (Sep 15, 2009): n/a.
Library Journal 134, no. 19. (Nov 15, 2009): 53.
Publishers Weekly 256, no. 16. (Apr 20, 2009): n/a.
Publishers Weekly 256, no. 39. (Sep 28, 2009): n/a.

The Hunger Games. **Suzanne Collins.** New York: Scholastic Press.
  2008. *The Hunger Games.*
  2009. *Catching Fire.*
  2010. *Mockingjay.*

DESCRIPTION: In a post-apocalyptic dystopia, two teens from each of the twelve districts of the nation of Panem are selected in a lottery to fight to the death in an arena. The battle is televised by the Capitol, which maintains strict control over the districts.

REASONS FOR CHALLENGES: anti-ethnic; anti-family; insensitivity; offensive language; occult/satanic; violence

AWARDS AND MEDIA CONNECTIONS

First film in a projected trilogy based on the book was released March 23, 2012. The film earned $152.5 million opening weekend, the second largest opening weekend gross in North America at that time.
Best Books for Young Adults, 2009.
Booklist Editor's Choice, 2008.
California Young Reader Medal, 2011.
Cybil Award Winner for fantasy and science-fiction, 2008.
Golden Duck Award in the Young Adult Fiction Category, 2009.
New York Times Notable Children's Book, 2008.
Publishers Weekly's Best Books of the Year, 2008.
Quick Picks for Reluctant Young Adult Readers, 2009.
School Library Journal Best Books, 2008.

REVIEWS

Booklist 105, no. 1. (Sep 1, 2008): 97.
Bulletin of the Center for Children's Books 62, no. 3. (Nov 2008): 112.
Entertainment Weekly, suppl. Fall TV Preview/Special Double Issue 1010/1011 (Sep 12, 2008): 139.
Horn Book Magazine 84, no. 5. (Sep/Oct 2008): 580.
Kirkus 17. (Sep 1, 2008): n/a.
New York Times Book Review (Nov 9, 2008): BR.30.
Publishers Weekly 255, no. 44 (Nov 3, 2008): n/a.
Publishers Weekly 256, no. 25 (Jun 22, 2009): n/a.
Time, suppl. Commemorative Issue 174, no. 9 (Sep 7, 2009): 65.

Sherman Alexie. *The Absolutely True Diary of a Part-Time Indian.* New York: Little, Brown, 2007.

DESCRIPTION: A semi-biographical novel about a young artist who chooses to leave his school on the Spokane Indian Reservation in the hopes of finding a better education at a white school. A coming-of-age tale examining how one teen tries to find his way without forgetting his past.

REASONS FOR CHALLENGES: offensive language; racism; religious viewpoint; sexually explicit; unsuited to age group

AWARDS AND MEDIA CONNECTIONS

American Indian Youth Literature Award, 2008.
Best Books for Young Adults Top Ten, 2008.
Boston-Globe Horn Book Award winner, 2008.
California Young Reader Medal winner, 2010.
Horn Book Fanfare, 2007.
International Book on Books for Young People Sweden—Peter Pan Prize winner, 2009.
Los Angeles Times Book Prize finalist, 2007.
National Book Award for Young People's Literature winner, 2007.
Odyssey winner for best audio book recording read by Sherman Alexie, 2009.

REVIEWS

Booklist 103, no. 22 (Aug 2007): 61.
Bulletin of the Center for Children's Books 61, no. 2 (Oct 2007): 72.
Entertainment Weekly, suppl. Special Double Issue/The Photo Issue 959/960 (Oct 19, 2007): 131.
Horn Book Magazine 83, no. 5 (Sep/Oct 2007): 563–564.
Kirkus 14 (Jul 15, 2007).
Los Angeles Times (Sep 16, 2007): R.5.
New York Times Book Review (Nov 11, 2007): 7.39.

Alice series. Phyllis Reynolds Naylor. New York: Atheneum.
1985. *The Agony of Alice.*
1989. *Alice in Rapture, Sort of.*
1991. *Reluctantly Alice.*
1992. *All But Alice.*

1993. *Alice in April.*
1994. *Alice In-Between.*
1995. *Alice the Brave.*
1996. *Alice in Lace.*
1997. *Outrageously Alice.*
1998. *Achingly Alice.*
1999. *Alice on the Outside.*
2000. *The Grooming of Alice.*
2001. *Alice Alone.*
2002. *Starting with Alice.*
2002. *Simply Alice.*
2003. *Alice in Blunderland.*
2003. *Patiently Alice.*
2004. *Lovingly Alice.*
2004. *Including Alice.*
2005. *Alice on Her Way.*
2006. *Alice in the Know.*
2007. *Dangerously Alice.*
2008. *Almost Alice.*
2009. *Intensely Alice.*
2010. *Alice in Charge.*
2011. *Incredibly Alice.*
2012. *Alice on Board.*
2013. *Always Alice.*

DESCRIPTION: This series chronicles the life of Alice McKinley from age 11 up through her university attendance. The series finale *Always Alice* covers her life from age 18 through 60. Three prequels tell the story of Alice's third, fourth, and fifth grade years. As Alice ages through the series, the books cover a wide variety of topics including teen pregnancy, parental infidelity, inappropriate teacher-student relationships, LGBTQ issues, racism, and loss of friendships.

REASONS FOR CHALLENGES: nudity; offensive language; religious viewpoint

AWARDS AND MEDIA CONNECTIONS
ALA Notable Books for Children, 1986. *The Agony of Alice.*
ALA Notable Books for Children, 1993. *All But Alice.*
Best Books for Young Adults, 1998. *Outrageously Alice.*

REVIEWS

Booklist 105, no. 17 (May 1, 2009): 78.
Booklist 107, no. 17 (May 1, 2011): 88.
Childhood Education 62, no. 4 (Mar 1986): 304.
Horn Book Magazine 85, no. 4 (Jul/Aug 2009): 428.
Horn Book Magazine 86, no. 4 (Jul/Aug 2010): 117.
Kirkus 8 (Apr 15, 2012). n/a.
Publishers Weekly 235, no. 6 (Feb 10, 1989): 72.
School Library Journal 58, no. 07 (Jul 2012): n/a.

Sonya Sones. *What My Mother Doesn't Know.* New York: Simon & Schuster Books for Young Readers, 2001.

DESCRIPTION: This novel told in verse is about the romantic and family life of high school freshman Sophie Stein. Sophie experiences relationships with different boys and learns the difference between love and lust.

REASONS FOR CHALLENGES: nudity; offensive language; sexually explicit

AWARDS AND MEDIA CONNECTIONS
Best Book for Young Adults, 2002.
Booklist Editor's Choice, 2001.
Iowa Teen Book Award winner, 2005.
International Reading Association Young Adults' Choice, 2003.
Michigan Thumbs Up Award Honor, 2002.
New York Public Library Book for the Teen Age, 2002, 2003, and 2004.
Pennsylvania Young Reader's Choice Award, Young Adult Recommended Title, 2003.
Top Ten Quick Pick for Reluctant Young Adult Readers, 2002.
Voice of Youth Advocates Top Shelf for Middle School Readers, 2003.

REVIEWS
The Book Report 20, no. 5 (Mar/Apr 2002): 51–52.
Booklist 98, no. 6 (Nov 15, 2001): 573.
Bulletin of the Center for Children's Books 55, no. 4 (Dec 2001): 152–153.
Entertainment Weekly 625/626 (Nov 16, 2001): 114.
Kirkus 18 (Sep 15, 2001). n/a.

New York Times Book Review (Sep 16, 2001): 7.26.

Publishers Weekly 248, no. 42 (Oct 15, 2001): 72.

School Library Journal 47, no. 10 (Oct 2001): 171–172.

Gossip Girl. **Cecily Von Ziegesar.** New York: Little, Brown.

2002. *Gossip Girl.*

2002. *You Know You Love Me.*

2003. *All I Want Is Everything.*

2003. *Because I'm Worth It.*

2004. *I Like It Like That.*

2004. *You're the One That I Want.*

2005. *Nobody Does It Better.*

2005. *Nothing Can Keep Us Together.*

2006. *Only in Your Dreams.*

2006. *Would I Lie to You?*

2007. *Don't You Forget About Me.*

2009. *I Will Always Love You.*

2007. *It Had To Be You: The Gossip Girl Prequel.*

DESCRIPTION: This series is about a group of privileged teens living in Manhattan's Upper East Side who visit an anonymous blog, "Gossip Girl," which spills rumors and gossip about the book's main characters. The series follows the glamorous lifestyles of the characters as they throw lavish parties, fall in and out of love, and worry about getting in to the Ivy League schools that would seem to be their birthright.

REASONS FOR CHALLENGES: drugs; offensive language; sexually explicit

AWARDS AND MEDIA CONNECTIONS

The books are the basis of the popular CW television series than ran for six seasons from 2007–2012. The books have spawned two spin-off novel series, *It Girl* and *Gossip Girls: The Carlyles.*

REVIEWS

Booklist 98, no. 19/20 (Jun 1/Jun 15, 2002): 1709–1710.

Booklist 102, no. 7 (Dec 1, 2005): 47.

Booklist 102, no. 22 (Aug 2006): 70.

Kirkus 8 (Apr 15, 2002). n/a.

Kirkus 16 (Aug 15, 2002). n/a.

Publishers Weekly 249, no. 3 (Jan 21, 2002): 91.
Publishers Weekly 249, no. 29 (Jul 22, 2002): 181–182.
School Library Journal 48, no. 6 (Jun 2002): 148.
School Library Journal 48, no. 10 (Oct 2002): 174.
School Library Journal 49, no. 8 (Aug 2003): 168.
School Library Journal 50, no. 2 (Feb 2004): 152.
Teen People 5, no. 4 (May 2002): 92.
YM 50, no. 6 (Jul 2002): 32.

Ellen Hopkins. *Crank.* New York: Simon Pulse, 2004.

DESCRIPTION: This novel in verse is a book loosely based on Hopkins's own daughter's addiction to crystal meth. Kristina, a good girl, tries meth for the first time on a trip to visit her father. The drug takes over Kristina's life as she spirals downward, becoming addicted and pregnant.

REASONS FOR CHALLENGES: drugs; offensive language; sexually explicit

AWARDS AND MEDIA CONNECTIONS
New York Times best seller.
Quick Picks for Reluctant Young Adult Readers, 2005.
Society of School Librarians International Honor, 2005.

REVIEWS
Booklist 101, no. 6 (Nov 15, 2004): 595.
Kirkus 19 (Oct 1, 2004).
Publishers Weekly 251, no. 44 (Nov 1, 2004): 63–64.
School Library Journal 50, no. 11 (Nov 2004): 145.

Natasha Friend. *Lush.* New York: Scholastic Press, 2006.

DESCRIPTION: Thirteen-year-old Samantha has an alcoholic father. Because she can't tell any of her friends her secret, she writes notes and inserts them into an unpopular library book. To her surprise, she begins to get written advice from a secret pen pal within the pages of the book. Meanwhile Sam finds that she's willing to do anything to get a boy at school to like her, even if it means drinking like her father.

REASONS FOR CHALLENGES: drugs; offensive language; sexually explicit; unsuited to age group

AWARDS AND MEDIA CONNECTIONS
International Reading Association Young Adult Choices, 2008.
Rhode Island Teen Book Award, 2008.
Quick Pick for Reluctant Young Adult Readers, 2007.

REVIEWS
Booklist 103, no. 5 (Nov 1, 2006): 41.
Bulletin of the Center for Children's Books 60, no. 5 (Jan 2007): n/a.
The Horn Book Guide to Children's and Young Adult Books 18, no. 1
    (Spring 2007): 87–107.
Kirkus 20 (Oct 15, 2006).

Amy Sonnie, editor. *Revolutionary Voices: A Multicultural Queer Youth Anthology.* Los Angeles: Alyson Books, 2000.

DESCRIPTION: An anthology of first-person prose, poetry, artwork, and performance pieces written by queer youth.

REASONS FOR CHALLENGES: homosexuality; sexually explicit

AWARDS AND MEDIA CONNECTIONS
Lambda Literary Awards best anthology/nonfiction finalist, 2001.
Lambda Literary Awards best children's/young adult finalist, 2001.
School Library Journal best adult books for high school students, 2001.

REVIEWS
The Advocate 825 (Nov 21, 2000): 58.
Booklist 97, no. 7 (Dec 1, 2000): 701.
Lambda Book Report 9, no. 3 (Oct 2000): 38–39.
School Library Journal 47, no. 2 (Feb 2001): 146.

Twilight, **Stephenie Meyer**. New York: Little, Brown.
    2005. *Twilight.*
    2006. *New Moon.*
    2007. *Eclipse.*
    2008. *Breaking Dawn.*

DESCRIPTION: When Bella leaves Phoenix to live with her father in Forks, Washington, she falls for a brooding classmate who is part of a vampire clan that does not prey on people. Over the course of the series, Bella and Edward fall in love, marry, and have a hybrid human/vampire baby. Edward turns Bella into a vampire to save her life and together they must battle to protect their child against ancient vampires that want to destroy her.

REASONS FOR CHALLENGES: religious viewpoint; violence

AWARDS AND MEDIA CONNECTIONS

The four books were turned into five films that have grossed over $5 billion dollars, breaking box office records and making Kristen Stewart, Robert Pattinson, and Taylor Lautner household names.

Best Books for Young Adults, 2006. *Twilight.*

Ten Best Books for Young Adults, 2006. *Twilight.*

Tennessee Volunteer State Book Award, 2007–2008. *Twilight.*

School Library Journal best books, 2005.

REVIEWS

Booklist 102, no. 21 (Jul 2006): 51.

Booklist 105, no. 1 (Sep 1, 2008): 88.

Bulletin of the Center for Children's Books 59, no. 4 (Dec 2005): 195.

The Horn Book Guide to Children's and Young Adult Books 17, no. 1 (Spring 2006): 88–102.

Kirkus 18 (Sep 15, 2005).

New York Times Book Review (Feb 12, 2006): 7.17.

New York Times Book Review (Aug 12, 2007): 7.19.

New York Times Book Review (Aug 17, 2008): BR.19.

Publishers Weekly 252, no. 28 (Jul 18, 2005): 207.

Publishers Weekly 253, no. 28 (Jul 17, 2006): 159.

Stephen Chobsky. *The Perks of Being a Wallflower.* New York: MTV/Gallery, 1999.

DESCRIPTION: An epistolary novel recounts the life and trials of Charlie, a high school freshman, to an unknown correspondent.

REASONS FOR CHALLENGES: anti-family; drugs; homosexuality; offensive language; religious viewpoint; sexually explicit; suicide; unsuited to age group

AWARDS AND MEDIA CONNECTIONS
Film released in 2012.
NPR's Top 100 Best Young Adult Novels.
Best Book for Young Adults, 2000.
Popular Paperbacks for Young Adults, 2002.
Quick Picks for Reluctant Readers, 2000.

REVIEWS
Booklist 95, no. 12 (Feb 1999): 1038.
Publishers Weekly 246, no. 4 (Jan 1999): 73.
School Library Journal 45, no. 6 (Jun 1999): 126.
Voice of Youth Advocates 31, no. 2: (Jun 2008): 107.

Harper Lee. *To Kill a Mockingbird*. Philadelphia: Lippincott, 1960.

DESCRIPTION: Set in the Deep South, the story is narrated by Scout, the daughter of Atticus Finch, a lawyer defending a black man accused of raping a white woman.

REASONS FOR CHALLENGES: offensive language; racism; unsuited to age group

AWARDS AND MEDIA CONNECTIONS
Sold more than 30 million copies in 40 different languages.
Library Journal named it "Best Novel of the 20th Century," 1999.
Oscar-winning film, 1962.
Pulitzer Prize, 1961.

REVIEWS
Atlantic, 206 (Aug 26, 1960): 98–99.
Christian Century, 78 (May 1961): 655.
Harper's (Aug 1960): 101.
Kirkus Review (May 1, 1960): 360.
New York Times Book Review, 65 (July 10, 1960): 5, 18.
New Yorker, 36 (Sept 10, 1960): 203–204.
Punch, 239 (Oct 26, 1960): 611–612.
Saturday Review, 43 (July 23, 1960): 15–16.
School Library Journal 85 (May 15, 1960): 44.
Time, 76 (Aug 1, 1960): 70–71.

J. D. Salinger. *The Catcher in the Rye.* Boston: Little, Brown, 1951.

DESCRIPTION: After being expelled from his prep school, Holden Caulfield spends a few days in New York City on his own.

REASONS FOR CHALLENGES: offensive language; sexually explicit; unsuited to age group

AWARDS AND MEDIA CONNECTIONS
One of *Modern Library*'s 100 Best English-language novels of the 20th century.
National Book Award Finalists, 1952.
One of *Time* magazine's 100 Best English-language novels since 1923.

REVIEWS
America. 85, no. 19 (Aug 11, 1951): 463–464.
Library Journal. 86 (July 1951): 1125–126.
Nation. 173, no. 9 (Sept 1951): 176.
New York Times. (Jul 15, 1951): n/a.
New York Times. (Jul 16, 1951): 19.

Carolyn Mackler. *The Earth, My Butt, and Other Big, Round Things.* Cambridge, MA: Candlewick, 2003.

DESCRIPTION: Virginia struggles to fit into her family, who are all smart, pretty, and thin, when her so-called perfect brother shatters her picture-perfect family image with a shocking call.

REASONS FOR CHALLENGES: offensive language; sexually explicit; unsuited to age group

AWARDS AND MEDIA CONNECTIONS
Books for the Teen Age, 2004.
Michael L. Printz Award for Excellence in Young Literature Honor Book, 2004.
Best Books for Young Adults, 1997.
Teen's Top Ten, 2004.

REVIEWS
Booklist 100, no.1 (Sept 2003): 115.
Horn Book Magazine 79, no. 5 (Sep/Oct 2003): 614–615.

Kirkus Reviews (June 2003): 861.
Kliatt (July 2003): 14.
Library Media Connection 22, no. 5 (Feb 2004): 72.
Publishers Weekly Reviews 250, no. 29 (July 2003): 197.
School Library Journal 49, no. 9 (Sept 2003): 218.

Robert Cormier. *The Chocolate War: A Novel.* New York: Pantheon, 1974.

DESCRIPTION: Jerry Renault refuses to participate in the school fund-raiser and is forced to defend himself and his convictions from his classmates.

REASONS FOR CHALLENGES: nudity; offensive language; sexually explicit; unsuited to age group

AWARDS AND MEDIA CONNECTIONS
Movie, 1988.
Robert Cormier is the 1991 Margaret A. Edwards Award for significant and lasting contribution to YA literature winner.
A *Kirkus Reviews* Choice, 1974
A *New York Times* Outstanding Books of the Year, 1974
A *School Library Journal* Best Books of the Year, 1974
School Library Journal's One Hundred Books That Shaped the Century, Jan 2000.
Best Book for Young Adults, 1974.
Best Books for Young Adults 1966–1999, Oct 2000.

REVIEWS
Booklist 71 (Mar 15, 1975): 747.
Kirkus Reviews 42 (Apr 1974): 371.
The Junior Bookshelf 39, no. 3 (Jun 1975): 194–195.
Library Journal 99 (May 1974): 1450.
Publishers Weekly 205 (Apr 15, 1974): 52.

Philip Pullman. *His Dark Materials* **trilogy.** New York: Alfred A. Knopf.
1996. *The Golden Compass.*
1997. *The Subtle Knife.*
2000. *The Amber Spyglass.*

DESCRIPTION: The epic fantasy series follows Lyra and Will as they cross multiple parallel universes delving into the mystery of Dust.

REASONS FOR CHALLENGES: political viewpoint; religious viewpoint; violence

AWARDS AND MEDIA CONNECTIONS

The Golden Compass Movie, 2007.

ALA *Notable Children's Books,* 1997.

Booklist Best of the Best One-Hundred, 2000.

Booklist Editors Choice, 1996.

Books for the Teen Age, 1997.

Books for the Teen Age, 2001.

Bulletin of the Center for Children's Books—1996 Blue Ribbon Awards.

Carnegie Medal for Children's Fiction, 1995. *The Golden Compass* in the UK.

Best Books for Young Adults, 1997.

Best Books for Young Adults, 2001.

Whitbread Book of the Year, 2001. *The Amber Spyglass.*

REVIEWS

The Amber Spyglass Review Sources

Book Report 19, no. 4 (Jan/Feb 2001): 57.

Fantasy & Science Fiction, 100, no. 4 (Apr 2001): 26–29.

Horn Book Magazine, 76, no. 6 (Nov/Dec 2000): 735–738.

Publishers Weekly 247, no. 39 (Sept 2000): 119.

School Library Journal 46, no. 10, (Oct 2000): 170.

The Golden Compass Review Sources

Book Report 15, no. 2 (Sept/Oct 1996): 43.

Booklist 92 no.13 (Mar 1996): 1179.

Horn Book Magazine 72, no. 4 (Jul/Aug 1996): 464–465.

Library Journal 121, no. 3 (Feb 1996): 176–177.

New York Times Book Review 145, no. 50432 (May 19, 1996): 34.

Publishers Weekly 243, no. 8 (Feb 19, 1996): 216.

School Library Journal 42, no. 4 (Apr 1996): 158.

The Subtle Knife Review Sources

Book Report 16, no. 4 (Jan/Feb 1998): 37.

Booklist 93, no. 21 (Jul 1997): 1818.

Horn Book Magazine 73, no. 5 (Sep/Oct 1997): 578–579.

New York Times Book Review 147, no. 51132 (Apr 19, 1998): 32.

Publishers Weekly 244, no. 26 (June 30, 1997): 77.

School Library Journal 43, no. 10 (Oct 1997): 137.

Charise Mericle Harper. *Flashcards of My Life: A Novel.* New York: Little, Brown, 2006.

DESCRIPTION: Emily uses journaling flashcards with themes like "kiss" and "regrets" to help figure out her junior high life and family.

REASONS FOR CHALLENGES: sexually explicit; unsuited to age group

REVIEWS
Booklist 102, no. 11 (Feb 1, 2006): 50.
Kirkus Reviews 74, no. 1 (Jan 1, 2006): 41.
Publishers Weekly 253, no. 2 (Jan 6, 2006): 54.
School Library Journal 52, no. 1 (Jan 2006): 133.
Voice of Youth Advocates 28, no. 6 (Feb 2006): 485.

Kevin Henkes. *Olive's Ocean.* New York: Greenwillow, 2003.

DESCRIPTION: A summer visit to her grandmother's cottage on Cape Cod gives Martha perspective on the death of a classmate and relationships with her grandmother and with the Manning boys.

REASONS FOR CHALLENGES: offensive language; sexually explicit

AWARDS AND MEDIA CONNECTIONS
Books for the Teen Age, 2004.
Newbery Honor Book, 2004.
Notable Children's Books, 2004.
Best Books for Young Adults, 2004.

REVIEWS
Booklist 100, no. 1 (Sept 1, 2003): 122.
Horn Book Magazine 79, no. 6 (Nov/Dec 2003): 745–747.
Kirkus Reviews 71, no. 13 (July 1, 2003): 911.
Library Media Connection 22, no. 6 (Mar 2004): 64.
Publishers Weekly 250, no. 33 (Aug 18, 2003): 80.
School Library Journal 49, no. 8 (Aug 2003): 160.
Voice of Youth Advocates 26, no. 5 (Dec 2003): 394.

Robie H. Harris. *It's Perfectly Normal: A Book about Changing Bodies, Growing Up, Sex, and Sexual Health.* Cambridge, Mass: Candlewick, 1994. (Note: there are more recent editions available.)

DESCRIPTION: An introduction to human sexuality for children and young teenagers.

REASONS FOR CHALLENGES: sex education; sexually explicit

AWARDS AND MEDIA CONNECTIONS
ALA's Notable Children's Book, 1995.
Horn Book/Boston Globe Book Awards, 1995.
New York Times, Notable Books of the Year, 1994.
Publishers Weekly Best Book of the Year, 1994.
Best Books for Young Adults, 1995.

REVIEWS
Booklist 91, no. 2 (Sept 15, 1994): 133.
Horn Book Magazine 71, no. 2 (Mar/Apr 1995): 214–215.
School Library Journal. 41, no. 3 (Mar 1995): 141.
Publishers Weekly 241, no. 45 (Nov 7, 1994): 44.
School Library Journal 40, no. 12 (Dec 1994): 123.
Voices of Youth Advocates Reviews (Dec 2009): n/a.

Chris Crutcher. *Athletic Shorts: Six Short Stories.* New York: Greenwillow, 1991.

DESCRIPTION: Six short stories about athletes and their lives.

REASONS FOR CHALLENGES: homosexuality; offensive language

AWARDS AND MEDIA CONNECTIONS
Booklist Best of the Best One-Hundred, 2000.
School Library Journal Best Books of the Year, 1991.
Best Books for Young Adults, 1992.
Best Books for Young Adults 1966–1999, Oct 2000.
Quick Picks for Reluctant Young Adult Readers, 1992.

REVIEWS
ALAN Review 19 (Fall 1991): 34.
Booklist 88 (Oct 15, 1991): 428.
Horn Book Magazine 67, no. 5 (Sep/Oct 1991): 602.
Publishers Weekly 238 (Aug 23, 1991): 278.

School Library Journal 37, no. 9 (Sep 1991): 278.
Voices of Youth Advocates 15 (Apr 1992): 26.

Judy Blume. *Forever . . . : A Novel.* Scarsdale, NY: Bradbury, 1975.

DESCRIPTION: Katherine and Michael's relationship and first sexual experiences are told in this groundbreaking novel, the first teen novel to portray sexual relations in a positive manner.

REASONS FOR CHALLENGES: offensive language; sexual content

AWARDS AND MEDIA CONNECTIONS
Booklist's Top One Hundred Countdown: Best of the Best Books for Young Adults, Oct 15, 1994.
Judy Blume is the 1996 Margaret A. Edwards Award for significant and lasting contribution to YA literature winner.
Popular Paperbacks for Young Adults, Sex is . . . list, 2008.

REVIEWS
Booklist 72 (Oct. 15, 1975): 291.
Junior Bookshelf 41, no. 1 (Feb 1977): 49.
School Library Journal 22, no. 3 (Nov 1975): 95.

Chris Crutcher. *Whale Talk.* New York: Greenwillow, 2001.

DESCRIPTION: T. J., a multiracial adopted teen, recruits the less popular students to join the new swim team.

REASONS FOR CHALLENGES: racism; offensive language

AWARDS AND MEDIA CONNECTIONS
Best Book for Young Adults, 2002.
Popular Paperbacks for Young Adults, 2005.
Top 10 Best Book for Young Adults, 2002.

REVIEWS
Book Report 20, no. 2 (Sep/Oct 2001): 60.
Bulletin of the Center for Children's Books (Apr 2001): n/a.
Horn Book Magazine 77, no. 3 (May/Jun 2001): 320–321.
Multicultural Review 10, no. 3 (Sep 2001): 114.
Publishers Weekly 248, no. 11 (Mar 12, 2001): 91.
School Library Journal 47 no. 5 (May 2001): 148.

Marilyn Reynolds. *Detour for Emmy.* Buena Park, CA: Morning Glory, 1993.

DESCRIPTION: Emmy struggles with the issues of teen motherhood with little support from family and none from the baby's father.

REASONS FOR CHALLENGES: sexual content

AWARDS AND MEDIA CONNECTIONS
Best Books for Young Adult Readers, 1994.

REVIEWS
Booklist (Oct 1, 1993): n/a.
Kirkus Reviews (Jul 15, 1993): n/a.
Publishers Weekly 240, no. 26 (June 28, 1993): 79.
School Library Journal 39, no. 7 (Jul 1993): 102.

Harry Potter. **J. K. Rowling.** New York: Arthur A. Levine.
1998. *Harry Potter and the Sorcerer's Stone.*
1999. *Harry Potter and the Chamber of Secrets.*
1999. *Harry Potter and the Prisoner of Azkaban.*
2000. *Harry Potter and the Goblet of Fire.*
2003. *Harry Potter and the Order of the Phoenix.*
2005. *Harry Potter and the Half-Blood Prince.*
2007. *Harry Potter and the Deathly Hallows.*

DESCRIPTION: The *Harry Potter* series chronicles the life and adventures of Harry Potter during his school time at Hogwarts School of Witchcraft and Wizardry and of his ongoing battle against the Dark Lord Voldemort.

REASONS FOR CHALLENGES: Occult/Satanism; violence; anti-family; religious viewpoint

AWARDS AND MEDIA CONNECTIONS
Movies of each book.
ALA's *Notable Children's Books.* Multiple titles.
Booklist Best of the Best One-Hundred, 2000. *Harry Potter and the Sorcerer's Stone.*
Booklist Editors Choice. Multiple titles.
Books for the Teen Age, 2004.

Bram Stoker Book Awards for Young Readers, 2004. *Harry Potter and the Order of the Phoenix.*

Hugo Award, 2001. *Harry Potter and the Goblet of Fire.*

New York Times Notable Books of the Year, 2000. *Harry Potter and the Goblet of Fire.*

New York Times Notable Books of the Year, 2007. *Harry Potter and the Deathly Hallows.*

Publishers Weekly's Best Books. Multiple titles.

School Library Journal Best Books of the Year. *Harry Potter and the Sorcerer's Stone and Harry Potter and the Chamber of Secrets.*

Whitbread Children's Book of the Year, 1999. *Harry Potter and the Prisoner of Azkaban.*

Best Books for Young Adults. Multiple titles.

Teen's Top Ten. Multiple titles.

REVIEWS

Harry Potter and the Sorcerer's Stone Reviews

Book Report 17, no. 5 (Mar/Apr 1999): 63.

Booklist 95, no. 2 (Sep 15, 1998): 230.

Horn Book Magazine 75, no. 1 (Jan/Feb 1999): 71.

New York Times Book Review 148, no. 51433 (Feb 14, 1999): 26.

Publishers Weekly 245, no. 29 (July 20, 1998): 220.

School Library Journal 44, no. 10 (Oct 1998): 145–146.

Harry Potter and the Chamber of Secrets Reviews

Book Report 18, no. 2 (Sep/Oct 1999): 62.

Booklist 95, no. 18 (May 15, 1999): 1690–1691.

Christian Science Monitor 91, no. 141 (June 17, 1999): 19.

Horn Book Magazine 75, no. 4 (Jul/Aug 1999): 472-473.

Publishers Weekly 246, no. 22 (May 31, 1999): 94.

School Library Journal 45, no. 7 (Jul 1999): 99.

Wall Street Journal 233, no. 123 (June 251999): W9.

Harry Potter and the Prisoner of Azkaban Reviews

Book Report 18, no. 3 (Nov/Dec 1999): 65.

Booklist 96, no. 1 (Sep 1, 1999): 127.

Christian Science Monitor 91, no. 209 (Sep 23, 1999): 21.

Horn Book Magazine 75, no. 6 (Nov/Dec 1999): 744–745.

New Statesman 128, no. 4444 (July 12, 1999): 47–48.

New York Times 148, no. 51642 (Sep 11, 1999): A10.

Publishers Weekly 246, no. 29 (July 19, 1999): 195.

Reading Time 43, no. 4 (Nov 1999): 26.

School Library Journal 45, no. 10 (Oct 1999): 158.

Harry Potter and the Goblet of Fire Reviews

Book Report 19, no. 3 (Nov/Dec 2000): 62.

Booklist 96, no. 22 (Aug 2000): 2128.

Christian Science Monitor 92, no. 162 (Jul 13, 2000): 21.

Fantasy & Science Fiction 99, no. 6 (Dec 2000): 27.

Horn Book Magazine 76, no. 6 (Nov/Dec 2000): 762–763.

New Statesman 129, no. 4495 (Jul 17, 2000): 54–55.

New York Times Book Review 149, no. 51458 (Jul 23, 2000): 114.

People 54, no. 4 (Jul 24, 2000): 43.

Publishers Weekly 247, no. 29 (Jul 17, 2000): 195.

Publishers Weekly 247, no. 30 (Jul 24, 2000): 32.

Harry Potter and the Order of the Phoenix Reviews

Booklist 99, no. 21 (Jul 1, 2003): 1842–1843.

Horn Book Magazine 79, no. 5 (Sep/Oct 2003): 619–620.

New Statesman 132, no. 4645 (Jul 7, 2003): 49–50.

New York Times Book Review 152, no. 52543 (Jul 13, 2003): 13.

People 60, no. 1 (Jul 7, 2003): 45.

Publishers Weekly 250, no. 26 (Jun 30, 2003): 79.

School Library Journal 49, no. 8 (Aug 2003): 165.

Voice of Youth Advocates 26, no.3 (Aug 2003): 240.

Harry Potter and the Half-Blood Prince Reviews

ALAN Review 33, no. 1 (Fall 2005): 39.

Booklist 101, no. 22 (Aug 1, 2005): 1948.

Entertainment Weekly no. 831 (Jul 25, 2005): 72.

Entertainment Weekly no. 856/857 (Dec 30, 2005): 151–153.

Horn Book Magazine 81, no. 5 (Sep/Oct 2005): 587–588.

Journal of Adolescent & Adult Literacy 49, no. 3 (Nov 2005): 250–251.

Kirkus Reviews 73, no. 15 (Aug 1, 2005): 800.

National Review 57, no. 16 (Sep 12, 2005): 48–49.

New Statesman 134, no. 4751 (Aug 1, 2005): 38.

New York Times 154, no. 53292, Section 7 (Jul 31, 2005): 12.

People 64, no. 5 (Aug 1, 2005): 43.

Publishers Weekly 252, no. 29 (Jul 25, 2005): 77.

School Library Journal 51, no. 9 (Sep 2005): 212–213.

Time 166, no. 4 (Jul 25, 2005): 62–63.

Voices from the Middle 13, no. 2 (Dec 2005): 65.

Voice of Youth Advocates 28, no. 4 (Oct 2005): 328.

Harry Potter and the Deathly Hallows Reviews

Booklist 103, no. 22 (Aug 1, 2007): 4.

Entertainment Weekly no. 948 (Aug 17, 2007): 30–34.

Horn Book Magazine 83, no. 5 (Sep/Oct 2007): 551–553.

Kirkus Reviews 75, no. 16 (Aug 15, 2007): 810.

Kirkus Reviews 75, no. 23, Special Section (Dec 1, 2007): 12.

New Statesman 136, no. 4855 (Jul 30, 2007): 54–55.

New York Times 156, no. 54010 (Jul 19, 2007): A20.

New York Times Book Review 157, no. 54146 (Dec 2, 2007): 59.

People 68, no. 6 (Aug 6, 2007): 45.

Publishers Weekly 254, no. 30 (Jul 30, 2007): 83.

School Library Journal 53, no. 9 (Sep 2007): 206–207.

Voice of Youth Advocates 30, no. 4 (Oct 2007): 349.

Source: ALA Office for Intellectual Freedom

THE VALUE OF YOUNG ADULT LITERATURE

by Michael Cart for YALSA

Adopted by YALSA's Board of Directors, January 2008

ABSTRACT: This White Paper will discuss the nature and evolution of young adult literature with particular emphasis on its current condition and its value to its intended readership. In discussing its increased viability as a body of critically lauded literature, it will also discuss its importance in meeting the life needs of young adults and its increasing value in enhancing adolescent literacy. It will conclude by affirming the Young Adult Library Services Association's commitment to evaluating, promoting, and supporting the most widespread availability possible of this literature to American youth.

BACKGROUND: The term "young adult literature" is inherently amorphous, for its constituent terms "young adult" and "literature" are dynamic, changing as culture and society—which provide their context—change. When the term first found common usage in the late 1960s, it referred to realistic fiction that was set in the real (as opposed to imagined), contemporary world and addressed problems, issues, and life circumstances of interest to young readers aged approximately 12–18. Such titles were issued by the children's book divisions of American publishers and were marketed to institutions—libraries and schools—that served such populations.

While some of this remains true today, much else has changed. In recent years, for example, the size of this population group has changed dramatically. Between 1990 and 2000 the number of persons between 12 and 19 soared to 32 million, a growth rate of 17 percent that significantly outpaced the growth of the rest of the population. The size of

this population segment has also increased as the conventional definition of "young adult" has expanded to include those as young as 10 and,
since the late 1990s, as old as 25.

"Literature," which traditionally meant fiction, has also expanded to
include new forms of literary—or narrative—nonfiction and new forms
of poetry, including novels and book-length works of nonfiction in
verse. The increasing importance of visual communication has begun
to expand this definition to include the pictorial, as well, especially
when offered in combination with text as in the case of picture books,
comics, and graphic novels and nonfiction.

As a result of these newly expansive terms, the numbers of books being published for this audience have similarly increased, perhaps by as
much as 25 percent, based on the number of titles being reviewed by a
leading journal. Similarly, industry analyst Albert Greco states that the
sale of young adult books increased by 23 percent from 1999 to 2005.

Though once dismissed as a genre consisting of little more than
problem novels and romances, young adult literature has, since the
mid-1990s, come of age as literature—literature that welcomes artistic
innovation, experimentation, and risk-taking.

Evidence of this is the establishment of the Michael L. Printz Award,
which YALSA presents annually to the author of the best young adult
book of the year, "best" being defined solely in terms of literary merit.
Further evidence is the extraordinary number of critically acclaimed
adult authors who have begun writing for young adults—authors like
Michael Chabon, Isabel Allende, Dale Peck, Julia Alvarez, T. C. Boyle,
Joyce Carol Oates, Francine Prose, and a host of others. As a result of
these and other innovations young adult literature has become one of
the most dynamic, creatively exciting areas of publishing.

POSITION: YALSA is acknowledging this growing diversity by expanding
the number of book-related awards and lists it presents and publishes.
Audio books and graphic novels are only two of the new areas that
YALSA is targeting. Meanwhile it continues to promote excellence in
the field through such established prizes as the Printz, ALEX, and Margaret A. Edwards Awards and such recommended lists as Best Books for
Young Adults and Quick Picks for Reluctant Young Adult Readers.

YALSA also acknowledges that whether one defines young adult literature narrowly or broadly, much of its value cannot be quantified but is to
be found in how it addresses the needs of its readers. Often described as
"developmental," these needs recognize that young adults are beings in

evolution, in search of self and identity; beings who are constantly growing and changing, morphing from the condition of childhood to that of adulthood. That period of passage called "young adulthood" is a unique part of life, distinguished by unique needs that are—at minimum—physical, intellectual, emotional, and societal in nature.

By addressing these needs, young adult literature is made valuable not only by its artistry but also by its relevance to the lives of its readers. And by addressing not only their needs but also their interests, the literature becomes a powerful inducement for them to read, another compelling reason to value it, especially at a time when adolescent literacy has become a critically important issue. The Alliance for Excellent Education has declared a "literacy crisis among middle and high school students" in the wake of research from the National Assessment of Educational Progress that finds 65 percent of graduating high school seniors and 71 percent of America's eighth graders are reading below grade level.

As literacy has become another developmental need of young adults, organizations like the International Reading Association and the National Council of Teachers of English have begun to recognize the imperative need for "a wide variety of reading material that they (young adults) can and want to read" (IRA), books that "should be self-selected and of high interest to the reader" (NCTE), young adult books, in short.

As a literature of relevance that meets developmental needs—including literacy skills—young adult literature also becomes a developmental *asset*, which YALSA's *New Directions for Library Service to Young Adults* defines as "a factor promoting positive teenage development." The independent, nonprofit Search Institute offers a framework of forty such developmental assets.

YALSA finds another of the chief values of young adult literature in its capacity to offer readers an opportunity to see themselves reflected in its pages. Young adulthood is, intrinsically, a period of tension. On the one hand young adults have an all-consuming need to belong. But on the other, they are also inherently solipsistic, regarding themselves as being unique, which—for them—is not cause for celebration but, rather, for despair. For to be unique is to be unlike one's peers, to be "other," in fact. And to be "other" is to not belong but, instead, to be outcast. Thus, to see oneself in the pages of a young adult book is to receive the reassurance that one is not alone after all, not other, not alien but, instead, a viable part of a larger community of beings who share a common humanity.

Another value of young adult literature is its capacity for fostering understanding, empathy, and compassion by offering vividly realized portraits of the lives—exterior and interior—of individuals who are *unlike* the reader. In this way young adult literature invites its readership to embrace the humanity it shares with those who—if not for the encounter in reading—might forever remain strangers or—worse—irredeemably "other."

Still another value of young adult literature is its capacity for telling its readers the truth, however disagreeable that may sometimes be, for in this way it equips readers for dealing with the realities of impending adulthood and for assuming the rights and responsibilities of citizenship.

By giving readers such a frame of reference, it also helps them to find role models, to make sense of the world they inhabit, to develop a personal philosophy of being, to determine what is right and, equally, what is wrong, to cultivate a personal sensibility. To, in other words, become civilized.

CONCLUSION: For all of these reasons the Young Adult Library Services Association values young adult literature, believes it is an indispensable part of public and school library collections, and regards it as essential to healthy youth development and the corollary development of healthy communities in which both youth and libraries can thrive.

REFERENCES

Alliance for Excellent Education. Press Center, http://al14ed.org/press_room. Accessed 9/28/07.

Cart, Michael. "Teens and the Future of Reading." *American Libraries*. October 2007.

Cart, Michael. "Young Adult Literature: The State of a Restless Art" in *Passions and Pleasures* by Michael Cart. Lanham, MD: The Scarecrow Press, 2007.

International Reading Association. "Adolescent Literacy." www.reading.org/resources/issues/positions_adolescent.html. Accessed 9/28/07.

Magazine Publishers of America. Teen Market Profile. www.magazine.org/content/files/teenprofile04.pdf (PDF file). Accessed 9/28/07.

NCTE. "A Call To Action." www.ncte.org. Accessed 9/28/07.

Patrick Jones for the Young Adult Library Services Association. *New Directions for Library Service to Young Adults*. Edited by Linda Waddle. Chicago: ALA, 2002.

Search Institute. www.search-institute.org.

YALSA'S COMPETENCIES FOR LIBRARIANS SERVING YOUTH
Young Adults Deserve the Best

USING THE COMPETENCIES

- Download the competencies in English (www.ala.org/yalsa/ files/guidelines/yadeservethebest_201.pdf) (PDF) or en Espanol (www.ala.org/yalsa/files/guidelines/yacompetencies/ competencias2010.pdf) (PDF).

- Download YALSA's Public Library Evaluation Tool, a complementary tool to determine the health of YA services in public libraries, and a series of fact sheets at the Evaluation Tool webpage (www.ala.org/yalsa/guidelines/yacompetencies/evaltool).

- Listen to a webinar about the competencies (free for YALSA members, login required at www.ala.org/yalsa/yalsamemonly/webinars/webinars or $19 for nonmembers at www.ala. org/Template.cfm?Section=olcast&Template=/Conference/ ConferenceList.cfm&ConferenceTypeCode=R, choose the course named "Back to Basics: Updated Guidelines for Everyday.")

- Buy Young Adults Deserve the Best: YALSA's Competencies in Action (www.alastore.ala.org/detail.aspx?ID=2905) by Sarah Flowers (ALA Editions, 2010).

THE COMPETENCIES

Updated January 2010

YALSA, a division of the ALA that supports library services to teens, developed these competencies for librarians who serve young adults. Individuals who demonstrate the knowledge and skills laid out in this document will be able to provide quality library service for and with teenagers. Institutions seeking to improve their overall service capacity and increase public value to their community are encouraged to adopt these competencies.

YALSA first developed these competencies in 1981, which were revised in 1998, 2003, and 2010. The competencies can be used as a tool to evaluate and improve service, a foundation for library school curriculum, a framework for staff training and a set of guiding principles for use when speaking out for the importance of services to teens in libraries.

Audiences for the competencies include:

- Library educators
- School and library administrators
- Graduate students
- Young adult specialists
- School librarians
- Library training coordinators
- Public library generalists
- Human resources directors
- Nonlibrary youth advocates and service providers

AREA I. LEADERSHIP AND PROFESSIONALISM

The librarian will be able to:

1. Develop and demonstrate leadership skills in identifying the unique needs of young adults and advocating for service excellence, including equitable funding and staffing levels relative to those provided for adults and children.
2. Develop and demonstrate a commitment to professionalism and ethical behavior.
3. Plan for personal and professional growth and career development.
4. Encourage young adults to become lifelong library users by helping them to discover what libraries offer, how to use library resources, and how libraries can assist them in actualizing their overall growth and development.
5. Develop and supervise formal youth participation, such as teen advisory groups, recruitment of teen volunteers, and opportunities for employment.
6. Model commitment to building assets in youth in order to develop healthy, successful young adults.

7. Implement mentoring methods to attract, develop, and train staff working with young adults.

AREA II. KNOWLEDGE OF CLIENT GROUP
The librarian will be able to:

1. Become familiar with the developmental needs of young adults in order to provide the most appropriate resources and services.
2. Keep up-to-date with popular culture and technological advances that interest young adults.
3. Demonstrate an understanding of, and a respect for, diverse cultural, religious, and ethnic values.
4. Identify and meet the needs of patrons with special needs.

AREA III. COMMUNICATION, MARKETING & OUTREACH
The librarian will be able to:

1. Form appropriate professional relationships with young adults, providing them with the assets, inputs and resiliency factors that they need to develop into caring, competent adults.
2. Develop relationships and partnerships with young adults, administrators and other youth-serving professionals in the community by establishing regular communication and by taking advantage of opportunities to meet in person.
3. Be an advocate for young adults and effectively promote the role of the library in serving young adults, demonstrating that the provision of services to this group can help young adults build assets, achieve success, and in turn, create a stronger community.
4. Design, implement, and evaluate a strategic marketing plan for promoting young adult services in the library, schools, youth-serving agencies and the community at large.
5. Demonstrate the capacity to articulate relationships between young adult services and the parent institution's core goals and mission.
6. Establish an environment in the library wherein all staff serve young adults with courtesy and respect, and all staff are encouraged to promote programs and services for young adults.

7. Identify young adult interests and groups underserved or not yet served by the library, including at-risk teens, those with disabilities, non-English speakers, etc., as well as those with special or niche interests.
8. Promote young adult library services directly to young adults through school visits, library tours, etc., and through engaging their parents, educators and other youth-serving community partners.

AREA IV. ADMINISTRATION

The librarian will be able to:

1. Develop a strategic plan for library service with young adults based on their unique needs.
2. Design and conduct a community analysis and needs assessment.
3. Apply research findings towards the development and improvement of young adult library services.
4. Design activities to involve young adults in planning and decision-making.
5. Develop, justify, administer, and evaluate a budget for young adult services.
6. Develop physical facilities dedicated to the achievement of young adult service goals.
7. Develop written policies that mandate the rights of young adults to equitable library service.
8. Design, implement, and evaluate an ongoing program of professional development for all staff, to encourage and inspire continual excellence in service to young adults.
9. Identify and defend resources (staff, materials, facilities, funding) that will improve library service to young adults.
10. Document young adult programs and activities so as to contribute to institutional and professional memory.
11. Develop and manage services that utilize the skills, talents, and resources of young adults in the school or community.

AREA V. KNOWLEDGE OF MATERIALS

The librarian will be able to:

1. Meet the informational and recreational needs of young adults through the development of an appropriate collection for all types of readers and nonreaders.

2. Develop a collection development policy that supports and reflect the needs and interests of young adults and is consistent with the parent institution's mission and policies.
3. Demonstrate a knowledge and appreciation of literature for and by young adults in traditional and emerging formats.
4. Develop a collection of materials from a broad range of selection sources, and for a variety of reading skill levels, that encompasses all appropriate formats, including, but not limited to, media that reflect varied and emerging technologies, and materials in languages other than English.
5. Serve as a knowledgeable resource to schools in the community as well as parents and caregivers on materials for young adults.

AREA VI. ACCESS TO INFORMATION
The librarian will be able to:
1. Organize physical and virtual collections to maximize easy, equitable, and independent access to information by young adults.
2. Utilize current merchandising and promotional techniques to attract and invite young adults to use the collection.
3. Provide access to specialized information (i.e., community resources, work by local youth, etc.).
4. Formally and informally instruct young adults in basic research skills, including how to find, evaluate, and use information effectively.
5. Be an active partner in the development and implementation of technology and electronic resources to ensure young adults' access to knowledge and information.
6. Maintain awareness of ongoing technological advances and how they can improve access to information for young adults.

AREA VII. SERVICES
The librarian will be able to:
1. Design, implement and evaluate programs and services within the framework of the library's strategic plan and based on the developmental needs of young adults and the public assets libraries represent, with young adult involvement whenever possible.

2. Identify and plan services with young adults in nontraditional settings, such as hospitals, home-school settings, alternative education, foster care programs, and detention facilities.
3. Provide a variety of informational and recreational services to meet the diverse needs and interests of young adults and to direct their own personal growth and development.
4. Continually identify trends and pop-culture interests of young people to inform, and direct their recreational collection and programming needs.
5. Instruct young adults in basic information gathering, research skills and information literacy skills—including those necessary to evaluate and use electronic information sources—to develop lifelong learning habits.
6. Actively involve young adults in planning and implementing services and programs for their age group through advisory boards, task forces, and by less formal means (i.e., surveys, one-on-one discussion, focus groups, etc.)
7. Create an environment that embraces the flexible and changing nature of young adults' entertainment, technological and informational needs.

CURRENT RESEARCH RELATED TO YOUNG ADULT SERVICES, 2006–2009
A Supplement Compiled by the YALSA Research Committee

THE YALSA RESEARCH COMMITTEE 2008–2009

Chair: Sandra Hughes-Hassell, Chapel Hill, NC

Eliza T. Dresang, Seattle, WA

Elizabeth Figa, Denton, TX

Jennifer Burek-Pierce, Iowa City, IA

Linda Steele, Johnson City, TN

Julie Yen, Urbana, IL

Joyce Giuliani, Alexandria, VA

Bell, M. A. (2008). Everybody else is doing it! MultiMedia & Internet@ Schools, 15(6), 38–40.

An online survey of school librarians and technology teachers about their Internet access at school revealed that almost half of 600 respondents could not even read blogs from school. The number who could create or participate in them was even more discouraging, with about 60 percent denied this access. This article shares some tactics for gaining access to the Internet, starting with the bandwagon ploy. The goal is to present some examples that can be used to help build cases supporting increased web access in schools and districts that are still dealing with very restrictive filters.

Franklin, R. E. (2008). A private [school] matter: The state of materials challenges in private college preparatory school libraries in the southeast United States. SLMR, 11. Available at www.ala.org/ala/mgrps/divs/aasl/ aaslpubsandjournals/slmrb/slmrcontents/volume11/franklin.cfm

Materials challenges and censorship occur often in public and private educational settings. Private schools and their library media centers are not subject to the First Amendment but research reported in this article examines the state of challenges to materials held in private schools' media centers in the southeast United States as a way to gauge the frequency and outcomes of materials challenges in these institutions. The study builds on previous research of challenges in public schools as a framework to examine the types of challenges to materials in private college preparatory school libraries in the southeast, the outcomes of the challenges, and the factors that influenced the outcome of the challenges.

Jaeger, P., & Yan, Z. (2009). One law with two outcomes: Comparing the implementation of CIPA in public libraries and schools. Information Technology and Libraries, 28(1), 6–14.
This paper explores the implications of Children's Internet Protection Act (CIPA) in terms of its effects on public libraries and public schools, individually and in tandem. Drawing from both library and education research, the paper examines the legal background and basis of CIPA, the current state of Internet access and levels of filtering in public libraries and public schools, the perceived value of CIPA, the perceived consequences of CIPA, the differences in levels of implementation of CIPA in public libraries and public schools, and the reasons for those dramatic differences. After an analysis of these issues within the greater policy context, the paper suggests research questions to help provide more data about the challenges and questions revealed in this analysis.

Jones, C. E. (2006). Female sexuality in young adult literature. Ph.D. dissertation, Illinois State University, United States—Illinois. Retrieved June 1, 2009, from Dissertations & Theses: Full Text database. (Publication No. AAT 3233938).
This dissertation explores the developments in treatments of sexual issues in young adult literature from 1970 to the early twenty-first century, focusing on female sexual agency and identity. Chapter IV examines pedagogical possibilities and strategies for bringing literary sexual issues into both high school and college classrooms. Focusing on the tensions between censorship and freedom of speech, the chapter explores the pedagogical, social, and ethical dilemmas surrounding non-curricular discussions of sexuality within the classroom.

Lukenbill, W. B., & Lukenbill, J. F. (2007). Censorship: What do school library specialists really know? A consideration of students' rights, the law and implications for a new education paradigm. SLMR, 10. Available at www.ala.org/ala/mgrps/divs/aasl/aaslpubsandjournals/slmrb/slmrcon tents/vol ume10/lukenbill_censorship.cfm
This study sought to determine the knowledge levels of a sample of school librarians concerning what they know about and how they support important court rulings that affect students' First Amendment rights. The study also sought to determine predictive behaviors of these librarians in protecting students' First Amendment rights. Basically the study found that the level of knowledge concerning legal rulings is low, but that school librarians in principle support students' rights to information, and that they are willing to advocate for those rights within the confines of their positions. Data also revealed that certain personal and demographic characteristics determine predicative behaviors. The study concludes with suggestions for redefining school librarianship education, emphasizing school library media specialists' professional responsibility to understand freedom of speech issues, laws, and court rulings.

Steadman, W. (2008). Evidence of student voices: Finding meaning in intellectual freedom. Knowledge Quest, 37(2), 44–48.
The author reports the results of an action research project focused on determining what 12th grade students think about intellectual freedom issues after instruction in freedom of speech and analysis of an independent censorship case study. During the two-week project, each student independently investigated the controversy surrounding a book from the American Library Association's list of the 100 Most Frequently Challenged Books. This exploratory analysis demonstrated that the unit of study met tangible learning objectives that had not been covered elsewhere in the curriculum. Data analysis revealed that the unit met tangible learning objectives not covered elsewhere in the curriculum and pointed out the need for a school-wide systematic approach to instruction in censorship and intellectual freedom issues valuable to 21st century learners.

INTERPRETATIONS OF ALA'S LIBRARY BILL OF RIGHTS

ACCESS FOR CHILDREN AND YOUNG ADULTS TO NONPRINT MATERIALS

An Interpretation of the Library Bill of Rights

Library collections of nonprint materials raise a number of intellectual freedom issues, especially regarding minors. Article V of the Library Bill of Rights states, "A person's right to use a library should not be denied or abridged because of origin, age, background, or views."

The American Library Association's principles protect minors' access to sound, images, data, games, software, and other content in all formats such as tapes, CDs, DVDs, music CDs, computer games, software, databases, and other emerging technologies. ALA's Free Access to Libraries for Minors: An *Interpretation* of the Library Bill of Rights states:

> . . . The "right to use a library" includes free access to, and unrestricted use of, all the services, materials, and facilities the library has to offer. Every restriction on access to, and use of, library resources, based solely on the chronological age, educational level, literacy skills, or legal emancipation of users violates Article V.
>
> . . . [P]arents—and only parents—have the right and responsibility to restrict access of their children—and only their children—to library resources. Parents who do not want their children to have access to certain library services, materials, or facilities should so advise their children. Librarians and library governing bodies cannot assume the role of parents or the functions of parental authority in the private relationship between parent and child.

Lack of access to information can be harmful to minors. Librarians and library governing bodies have a public and professional obligation to ensure that all members of the community they serve have free, equal, and equitable access to the entire range of library resources regardless of content, approach, format, or amount of detail. This principle of library service applies equally to all users, minors as well as adults. Librarians and library governing bodies must uphold this principle in order to provide adequate and effective service to minors.

Policies that set minimum age limits for access to any nonprint materials or information technology, with or without parental permission, abridge library use for minors. Age limits based on the cost of the materials are also unacceptable. Librarians, when dealing with minors, should apply the same standards to circulation of nonprint materials as are applied to books and other print materials except when directly and specifically prohibited by law.

Recognizing that librarians cannot act *in loco parentis*, ALA acknowledges and supports the exercise by parents of their responsibility to guide their own children's reading and viewing. Libraries should provide published reviews or reference works that contain information about the content, subject matter, and recommended audiences for nonprint materials. These resources will assist parents in guiding their children without implicating the library in censorship.

In some cases, commercial content ratings, such as the Motion Picture Association of America (MPAA) movie ratings, might appear on the packaging or promotional materials provided by producers or distributors. However, marking out or removing this information from materials or packaging constitutes expurgation or censorship.

MPAA movie ratings, Entertainment Software Rating Board (ESRB) game ratings, and other rating services are private advisory codes and have no legal standing (Expurgation of Library Materials). For the library to add ratings to nonprint materials if they are not already there is unacceptable. It is also unacceptable to post a list of such ratings with a collection or to use them in circulation policies or other procedures. These uses constitute labeling, "an attempt to prejudice attitudes" (Labels and Rating Systems), and are forms of censorship. The application of locally generated ratings schemes intended to provide content warnings to library users is also inconsistent with the Library Bill of Rights.

The interests of young people, like those of adults, are not limited by subject, theme, or level of sophistication. Librarians have a responsibility to ensure young people's access to materials and services that reflect diversity of content and format sufficient to meet their needs.

Adopted June 28, 1989, by the ALA Council; amended June 30, 2004. [ISBN 8389–7351–5]

ACCESS TO RESOURCES AND SERVICES IN THE SCHOOL LIBRARY MEDIA PROGRAM

An Interpretation of the Library Bill of Rights

The school library media program plays a unique role in promoting intellectual freedom. It serves as a point of voluntary access to information and ideas and as a learning laboratory for students as they acquire critical thinking and problem-solving skills needed in a pluralistic society. Although the educational level and program of the school necessarily shape the resources and services of a school library media program, the principles of the Library Bill of Rights apply equally to all libraries, including school library media programs. Under these principles, all students have equitable access to library facilities, resources, and instructional programs.

School library media specialists assume a leadership role in promoting the principles of intellectual freedom within the school by providing resources and services that create and sustain an atmosphere of free inquiry. School library media specialists work closely with teachers to integrate instructional activities in classroom units designed to equip students to locate, evaluate, and use a broad range of ideas effectively. Intellectual freedom is fostered by educating students in the use of critical thinking skills to empower them to pursue free inquiry responsibly and independently. Through resources, programming, and educational processes, students and teachers experience the free and robust debate characteristic of a democratic society.

School library media specialists cooperate with other individuals in building collections of resources that meet the needs as well as the developmental and maturity levels of students. These collections provide resources that support the mission of the school district and are consistent with its philosophy, goals, and objectives. Resources in school library media collections are an integral component of the curriculum and represent diverse points of view on both current and historical issues. These resources include materials that support the intellectual growth, personal development, individual interests, and recreational needs of students.

While English is, by history and tradition, the customary language of the United States, the languages in use in any given community may vary. Schools serving communities in which other languages are used make efforts to accommodate the needs of students for whom English is a second language. To support these efforts, and to ensure equitable access to resources and services, the school library media program provides resources that reflect the linguistic pluralism of the community.

Members of the school community involved in the collection development process employ educational criteria to select resources unfettered by their personal, political, social, or religious views. Students and educators served by the school library media program have access to resources and services free of constraints resulting from personal, partisan, or doctrinal disapproval. School library media specialists resist efforts by individuals or groups to define what is appropriate for all students or teachers to read, view, hear, or access via electronic means.

Major barriers between students and resources include but are not limited to imposing age, grade-level, or reading-level restrictions on the use of resources; limiting the use of interlibrary loan and access to electronic information; charging fees for information in specific formats; requiring permission from parents or teachers; establishing restricted shelves or closed collections; and labeling. Policies, procedures, and rules related to the use of resources and services support free and open access to information.

It is the responsibility of the governing board to adopt policies that guarantee students access to a broad range of ideas. These include policies on collection development and procedures for the review of resources about which concerns have been raised. Such policies, developed by persons in the school community, provide for a timely and fair hearing and assure that procedures are applied equitably to all expressions of concern. It is the responsibility of school library media specialists to implement district policies and procedures in the school to ensure equitable access to resources and services for all students.

Adopted July 2, 1986, by the ALA Council; amended January 10, 1990; July 12, 2000; January 19, 2005; July 2, 2008. [ISBN 8389–7053–2]

MINORS AND INTERNET INTERACTIVITY

An Interpretation of the Library Bill of Rights

The digital environment offers opportunities for accessing, creating, and sharing information. The rights of minors to retrieve, interact with, and create information posted on the Internet in schools and libraries are extensions of their First Amendment rights. (See also other interpretations of the Library Bill of Rights, including "Access to Digital Information, Services, and Networks," "Free Access to Libraries for Minors," and "Access for Children and Young Adults to Nonprint Materials.")

Academic pursuits of minors can be strengthened with the use of interactive web tools, allowing young people to create documents and share them online; upload pictures, videos, and graphic material; revise public documents; and add tags to online content to classify and organize information. Instances of inappropriate use of such academic tools should be addressed as individual behavior issues, not as justification for restricting or banning access to interactive technology. Schools and libraries should ensure that institutional environments offer opportunities for students to use interactive web tools constructively in their academic pursuits, as the benefits of shared learning are well documented.

Personal interactions of minors can be enhanced by social tools available through the Internet. Social networking websites allow the creation of online communities that feature an open exchange of information in various forms, such as images, videos, blog posts, and discussions about common interests. Interactive web tools help children and young adults learn about and organize social, civic, and extracurricular activities. Many interactive sites invite users to establish online identities, share personal information, create web content, and join social networks. Parents and guardians play a critical role in preparing their children for participation in online activity by communicating their personal family values and by monitoring their children's use of the Internet. Parents and guardians are responsible for what their children—and only their children—access on the Internet in libraries.

The use of interactive web tools poses two competing intellectual freedom issues—the protection of minors' privacy and the right of free speech. Some have expressed concerns regarding what they perceive is an increased vulnerability of young people in the online environment when they use interactive sites to post personally identifiable information. In an effort to protect minors' privacy, adults sometimes restrict access to interactive web environments. Filters, for example, are sometimes used to restrict access by youth to interactive social networking tools, but at the same time deny minors' rights to free expression on the Internet. Prohibiting children and young adults from using social networking sites does not teach safe behavior and leaves youth without the necessary knowledge and skills to protect their privacy or engage in responsible speech. Instead of restricting or denying access to the Internet, librarians and teachers should educate minors to participate responsibly, ethically, and safely.

The First Amendment applies to speech created by minors on interactive sites. Usage of these social networking sites in a school or library allows minors to access and create resources that fulfill their interests and needs for information, for social connection with peers, and for participation in a community of learners. Restricting expression and access to interactive websites because the sites provide tools for sharing information with others violates the tenets of the Library Bill of Rights. It is the responsibility of librarians and educators to monitor threats to the intellectual freedom of minors and to advocate for extending access to interactive applications on the Internet.

As defenders of intellectual freedom and the First Amendment, libraries and librarians have a responsibility to offer unrestricted access to Internet interactivity in accordance with local, state, and federal laws and to advocate for greater access where it is abridged. School and library professionals should work closely with young people to help them learn skills and attitudes that will prepare them to be responsible, effective, and productive communicators in a free society.

Adopted July 15, 2009, by the ALA Council.

LABELING AND RATING SYSTEMS

An Interpretation of the Library Bill of Rights

Libraries do not advocate the ideas found in their collections or in resources accessible through the library. The presence of books and other resources in a library does not indicate endorsement of their contents by the library. Likewise, providing access to digital information does not indicate endorsement or approval of that information by the library. Labeling and rating systems present distinct challenges to these intellectual freedom principles.

Labels on library materials may be viewpoint-neutral directional aids designed to save the time of users, or they may be attempts to prejudice or discourage users or restrict their access to materials. When labeling is an attempt to prejudice attitudes, it is a censor's tool. The American Library Association opposes labeling as a means of predisposing people's attitudes toward library materials.

Prejudicial labels are designed to restrict access, based on a value judgment that the content, language, or themes of the material, or the background or views of the creator(s) of the material, render it inappropriate or offensive for all or certain groups of users. The prejudicial label is used to warn, discourage, or prohibit users or certain groups of users from accessing the material. Such labels sometimes are used to place materials in restricted locations where access depends on staff intervention.

Viewpoint-neutral directional aids facilitate access by making it easier for users to locate materials. The materials are housed on open shelves and are equally accessible to all users, who may choose to consult or ignore the directional aids at their own discretion.

Directional aids can have the effect of prejudicial labels when their implementation becomes proscriptive rather than descriptive. When directional aids are used to forbid access or to suggest moral or doctrinal endorsement, the effect is the same as prejudicial labeling.

Many organizations use rating systems as a means of advising either their members or the general public regarding the organizations' opinions of the contents and suitability or appropriate age for use of certain books, films, recordings, websites, games, or other materials. The adoption, enforcement, or endorsement of any of these rating systems by a library violates the Library Bill of Rights. When requested, librarians should provide information about rating systems equitably, regardless of viewpoint.

Adopting such systems into law or library policy may be unconstitutional. If labeling or rating systems are mandated by law, the library should seek legal advice regarding the law's applicability to library operations.

Libraries sometimes acquire resources that include ratings as part of their packaging. Librarians should not endorse the inclusion of such rating systems; however, removing or destroying the ratings—if placed there by, or with permission of, the copyright holder—could constitute expurgation. In addition, the inclusion of ratings on bibliographic records in library catalogs is a violation of the Library Bill of Rights.

Prejudicial labeling and ratings presuppose the existence of individuals or groups with wisdom to determine by authority what is appropriate or inappropriate for others. They presuppose that individuals must be directed in making up their minds about the ideas they examine. The American Library Association affirms the rights of individuals to form their own opinions about resources they choose to read or view.

Adopted July 13, 1951, by the ALA Council; amended June 25, 1971; July 1, 1981; June 26, 1990; January 19, 2005; July 15, 2009.

INDEX

C